CU01510116

'Many fund managers think companies that take a long-term view are just not exciting enough. On one of my first visits to a fund manager, I was told that companies such as Delcam, which follow this approach, are "rather boring". Thankfully there are other genuine, patient, long-term investors like Lord Lee who appreciate "proper" companies like Delcam, which invests heavily in R&D, has grown steadily and pays a regular dividend. It has been a great pleasure to have him as an investor.'

Clive Martell, CEO, Delcam

'John Lee has been a long-standing investor in Treatt, having first bought into the company in 1999, and he remains a significant shareholder to this day. John is a very patient investor who understands the importance of long-term thinking in a business and I have always enjoyed the fact that John clearly understands our business, having followed us closely over many years. Frankly, we could not wish for a more supportive shareholder.'

Richard Hope, Group Finance Director, Treatt

How to Make a
Million – Slowly

PEARSON

At Pearson, we believe in learning – all kinds of learning for all kinds of people. Whether it's at home, in the classroom or in the workplace, learning is the key to improving our life chances.

That's why we're working with leading authors to bring you the latest thinking and best practices, so you can get better at the things that are important to you. You can learn on the page or on the move, and with content that's always crafted to help you understand quickly and apply what you've learned.

If you want to upgrade your personal skills or accelerate your career, become a more effective leader or more powerful communicator, discover new opportunities or simply find more inspiration, we can help you make progress in your work and life.

Pearson is the world's leading learning company. Our portfolio includes the Financial Times and our education business, Pearson International.

Every day our work helps learning flourish, and wherever learning flourishes, so do people.

To learn more, please visit us at **www.pearson.com/uk**

The Financial Times

With a worldwide network of highly respected journalists, *The Financial Times* provides global business news, insightful opinion and expert analysis of business, finance and politics. With over 500 journalists reporting from 50 countries worldwide, our in-depth coverage of international news is objectively reported and analysed from an independent, global perspective.

To find out more, visit **www.ft.com/pearsonoffer/**

How to Make a Million – Slowly

My Guiding Principles from a Lifetime of Successful Investing

John Lee

Harlow, England • London • New York • Boston • San Francisco • Toronto • Sydney
Auckland • Singapore • Hong Kong • Tokyo • Seoul • Taipei • New Delhi
Cape Town • São Paulo • Mexico City • Madrid • Amsterdam • Munich • Paris • Milan

PEARSON EDUCATION LIMITED
Edinburgh Gate
Harlow CM20 2JE
United Kingdom
Tel: +44 (0)1279 623623
Web: www.pearson.com/uk

First published 2014 (print and electronic)

ISBN: 978-1-292-00508-9 (print)
       978-1-292-00512-6 (PDF)
       978-1-292-00511-9 (ePub)
       978-1-292-00513-3 (eText)

British Library Cataloguing-in-Publication Data
A catalogue record for the print edition is available from the British Library

Library of Congress Cataloging-in-Publication Data
Lee, John, 1942 June 21-
 How to make a million--slowly : my guiding principles from a lifetime of successful investing /
John Lee.
   pages cm
 Includes index.
 ISBN 978-1-292-00508-9 (print) -- ISBN 978-1-292-00512-6 (PDF) -- ISBN 978-1-292-00511-9
 (ePub) -- ISBN 978-1-292-00513-3 (eText)
 1. Portfolio management. 2. Stocks. 3. Investment analysis. 4. Investments. I. Title.
 HG4529.5.L44 2014
 332.6--dc23
                                    2013035299

10 9 8 7 6 5 4 3
17 16 15 14

Cover design by Kit Foster, cover image © MURAT YILMAZ/Shutterstock.com

Print edition typeset in 9/13pt Stone Serif ITC by 30
Print edition printed and bound in Great Britain by Henry Ling, at the Dorset Press, Dorchester, Dorset

NOTE THAT ANY PAGE CROSS REFERENCES REFER TO THE PRINT EDITION

For Monique, Debbie and Elspeth, who never resented the time I devoted to my investment activities and are now hopefully appreciating the dividends

Contents

About the author

John Lee was born in Manchester in 1942, the son of a family doctor father and child psychologist mother. After qualifying as a chartered accountant and spending a period in stockbroking, he established a company specialising in amalgamations and mergers, which developed into a small public investment banking group. He was elected as a Conservative Member of Parliament in 1979, spending 13 years in the House of Commons, including six years as a Minister in Defence, Employment and Tourism. Following his defeat in the 1992 election he chaired the Christie Hospital NHS Trust and the Museum of Science and Industry in Manchester, becoming High Sheriff of Greater Manchester in 1998–9. In 2006 he was created a Life Peer – Lord Lee of Trafford – and currently sits in the House of Lords as a Liberal Democrat.

For more than 50 years John has been a serious private investor, having bought his first shares at the age of 15. For more than a decade he wrote his 'My Portfolio' column for *FT Money*, resulting in over 200 articles for the *Financial Times*. In December 2003 he disclosed that his PEP/ISA portfolio was worth £1 million, from £126,000 invested. It has since grown significantly. Over the years John has been on the boards of a number of public and private companies.

Acknowledgements

My grateful thanks to Christopher, Emma, Lucy and Anna, and all the team at FT Publishing for all their encouragement and support. Also to my indispensable secretary, Kathy, for all the typing, collation and assistance.

Thanks also to all those individuals – colleagues, readers and friends – who, over my lifetime of investing, have shared and trusted me with their ideas, thoughts and investment problems. To those who have benefited from my suggestions and recommendations, well done and good luck! To those who have suffered from my misjudgements and mistakes, I can only apologise.

Publisher's acknowledgements

We are grateful to the following for permission to reproduce copyright material:

Figures

Figures on pages 29, 38 and 48 from Lipper, a Thomson Reuters company; Figure on page 32 from Plenty of potential in store, *Financial Times*, 24/03/2000 (Lee, J.), © The Financial Times Limited. All Rights Reserved; Figure on page 46 with permission from Pochin's PLC; Figure on page 57 from Company REFS, May 2013, JD Financial Publishing Ltd; Figure on page 101 from Fidessa; Figure on page 109 from Patiently waiting for the endgame, *Financial Times*, 07/10/2006 (Lee, J.), © The Financial Times Limited. All Rights Reserved; Figure on page 123 from All aboard for growth at the new Fisher, *Financial Times*, 28/10/2000 (Lee, J.), © The Financial Times Limited. All Rights Reserved.

Text

Article on page 26 from New fizz from the kings of Vimto, *Financial Times*, 23/04/2000 (Lee, J.); Article on page 30 from Dicing with dividends, *Financial Times*, 07/03/2009 (Lee, J.); Article on page 32 from Plenty of potential in store, *Financial Times*, 24/03/2000 (Lee, J.); Article on page 34 from Family values at a discount, *Financial Times*, 02/10/2011 (Lee, J.); Article on page 36 from Share prices can belie true value, *Financial Times*, 05/05/2012 (Lee, J.); Article on page 39 from Misunderstood and undervalued, *Financial Times*, 05/03/2011 (Lee, J.); Article on page 42 from Unloved, unwanted and undervalued, *Financial Times*, 25/03/2000 (Lee, J.); Article on page 49 from Shareholder stamina for a long haul, *Financial Times*, 01/03/2008 (Lee, J.); Article on page 58 from Take your direction from the directors, *Financial Times*, 11/12/1999 (Lee, J.); Article on page 60 from Hardly a fool or a knave in sight, *Financial Times*, 01/06/2002 (Lee, J.); Article on page 62 from Read their lips and accounts, *Financial Times*, 16/06/2001 (Lee, J.); Article on page 64 from A good prospect on paper, *Financial Times*, 02/04/2005 (Lee, J.); Article on page 66 from Raise a glass to a solid earner, *Financial Times*, 03/03/2012 (Lee, J.); Article on page 68 from Anpario provides some food for thought, *Financial Times*, 01/09/2012 (Lee, J.); Article on page 70 from Time at an AGM is time well spent, *Financial Times*, 15/05/1999 (Lee, J.); Article on page 72 from At least I made the buffet, *Financial Times*, 15/02/2003 (Lee, J.); Article on page 89 from Investment lessons in a tough school, *Financial Times*, 13/05/2000 (Lee, J.); Article on page 91 from Profit-taking with a catch, *Financial Times*, 03/04/2004 (Lee, J.); Article on page 94 from Jewellery shares acquire extra sparkle, *Financial Times*, 05/08/2000 (Lee, J.); Article on page 96 from Tailored for both comfort and fit, *Financial Times*, 31/07/1999 (Lee, J.); Article on page 98 from On the scent of success at Jasmin, *Financial Times*, 09/09/2000 (Lee, J.); Article on page 107 from Years of patience pay off with Pifco, *Financial Times*, 26/05/2001 (Lee, J.); Article on page 109 from Patiently waiting for the end-game, *Financial Times*, 07/10/2006 (Lee, J.); Article on page 112 from Property has provided me with firm foundations, *Financial Times*, 07/11/2009

(Lee, J.); Article on page 115 from Windsor brings a touch of class, *Financial Times*, 02/03/2002 (Lee, J.); Article on page 120 from Proof I'm in it for the long haul, *Financial Times*, 06/10/2012 (Lee, J.); Article on page 123 from All aboard for growth at the new Fisher, *Financial Times*, 28/10/2000 (Lee, J.); Article on page 127 from How I made £1m from £126,200, *Financial Times*, 20/12/2003 (Lee, J.); Article on page 130 from How can I do what he's done?, *Financial Times*, 21/12/2003 (Warwick-Ching, L.).

In some instances we have been unable to trace the owners of copyright material, and we would appreciate any information that would enable us to do so.

Foreword

The stock market has had a bad time of it over the past decade. After a dot-com bust in the early noughties and a banking crisis eight years later, many people view it as a casino, populated by spivs and charlatans. Or they assume that you need to be a rocket scientist to exploit whatever opportunity it offers. The seemingly easy gains made just from buying and selling houses have only added to the disinterest.

But despite the ups and downs of recent years, shares are unquestionably the best vehicle for long-term savings. Unlike property, they are quick and easy to buy and sell. Unlike bonds, the income they generate through dividends can and usually does rise with inflation. Since the start of the twentieth century, shares have on average returned around 5% a year after allowing for inflation.

Smaller shares have generally done better still. They are more likely to be ignored by big investors, yet more likely to grow rapidly, and more likely to be taken over at a big premium. It's no coincidence that some of the UK's most successful fund managers – people like Harry Nimmo at Standard Life, Gervais Williams at Miton and Giles Hargreave at Marlborough – operate in the small cap arena.

They offer superior returns because they are riskier, and managing that risk is crucial to maximising profits. You could argue that Lord Lee, with his background in accountancy and long spells in the boardrooms of quoted companies, has an edge that ordinary investors will struggle to replicate.

But most of his advice is based not on inside knowledge or technical expertise but on common sense. He looks for companies with strong finances, committed managers and improving outlooks – and buys their shares when they are attractive prices. Then he waits, for years if necessary. This is essentially the same approach followed by legendary value investors such as Warren Buffett and Benjamin Graham. It worked in the US back in the 1930s, and it works in the UK now. With patience, method and discipline, anyone can do it.

How to Make a Million – Slowly is a very frank and personal story. John's successes and his mistakes – which make an absorbing and informative read – are a must for every private investor.

Jonathan Eley
Editor, FT Money
July 2013

Introduction

There are three main parts of my life: family, the stock market and politics. This book is focused on the stock market – more than 50 years of a fascinating hobby: from my first investment aged 15, through to becoming what I like to describe as 'a serious private investor'. This period also included the more recent dozen years of writing the 'My Portfolio' column in *FT Money* (more than 200 articles).

I wrote this book because I want to share with you my investing principles from the last 50 years. As I was writing it I looked back over that time at all my transactions, many hundreds of them; sometimes it feels as if I have owned every quoted share! I have made many mistakes – I share these with honesty and in some cases painful embarrassment, but I have learned from the negatives and because of this there have been more successes than failures. This book takes the interested or potential private investor through my years of investing – the gains and the losses, the anecdotes and the experiences. The book details my guiding principles.

One key point that I want to emphasise is that you don't need to be wealthy to invest. I started with little capital – my first shares cost £45 in 1957 and the experience was a total disaster. Today I have many individual holdings worth £100,000+. An article in the *Financial Times* in December 2003 disclosed that my Individual Savings Account (ISA) had grown by then to more than £1 million in value – pleasingly, since then it has progressed further.

I have called the book *How to Make a Million – Slowly* because it sums up my approach to stock market success – building up a portfolio brick by brick, share by share over many years. I believe the long-term holding of shares in UK PLCs is something that is worthwhile in a broader national context. There are those who treat the stock market as a casino – constantly dealing in and out – usually not knowing or caring what activities the companies they buy and sell are engaged in. Good luck to them – that is their choice – but it is not my way. Nor do I believe that day trading such as this is the way to success for most people. I like to get to know and understand the companies I invest in – I feel proud to own a small part of many fine businesses.

I have included a small number of my *Financial Times* articles which have been published in the past 15 years. I've done this because they illustrate well my investing philosophy. Looking back at these articles I'm pleased – and sometimes surprised – at the ongoing relevance of my writings, although there have been some avoidable howlers. Although the companies may have changed, the principles in these extracts remain relevant for today's investor.

In this book I have distilled a number of key investing lessons which I have developed over the years – hopefully private investors will find them useful. You learn about dividend yields, price earnings ratios, avoiding losses and 'when to sell'. I explain my approach and draw out my thoughts and conclusions.

I hope others get the same pleasure from their stock market investing as I have, and that they benefit from my scars and my successes. Common sense and above all patience are the keys to building *your* fortune.

Yearly performance round-up

Capital performance

	My capital performance (%)	FTSE 100 (%)	FTSE Small Cap (%)
2001	+5	–16.15	–18.98
2002	+5	–24.48	–29.41
2003	+44	+13.62	+35.95
2004	+30	+7.54	+11.43
2005	+20	+16.71	+19.85
2006	+18	+10.71	+18.15
2007	–14	+3.8	–12.43
2008	–42	–31.33	–45.79
2009	+28	+22.07	+49.76
2010	+29	+9	+16.27
2011	–2	–5.55	–14.86
2012	+24	+5.84	+24.39

2001 +5%

'2001 was a most difficult year but there were opportunities amid the gloom.'

A year of foot and mouth disease, the September 11th terrorist attacks, and the profits warnings of a deteriorating economy. Highlight was the takeover of electrical appliances company Pifco, a major holding, followed by a nice Christmas present with the takeover of electronics TGI by a private Danish company; otherwise nothing of note – a year of swings and roundabouts.

2002 +5%

'Given the brutal market of 2002 and a dearth of corporate activity I am well satisfied with 5% capital growth.'

This year's 'stars' have been James Fisher in shipping services, Lookers the motor retailer, NWF in animal feeds/foods and fuel distribution – all with profits growth and an upward rating. On the negative side my only disaster has been Abbeycrest, the jewellery manufacturer and distributor, where management has been struggling to cope with a range of problems.

2003 +44%

'A near 50% total investment return – to be precise, 44% capital growth plus 4.5% dividend income, and breaking through the £1 million PEP/ISA barrier makes 2003 a vintage year for me and my investment philosophy.'

Modest losses taken on enameller Bilston & Battersea, software specialist Jasmin, and air filtration company McLeod Russel, but a whole string of substantial successes with Christie, Clarkson, Parkdean Holidays and Windsor. Useful management buyout (MBO) profits from Jarvis Hotels and bed manufacturer Silentnight – both personal equity plan (PEP) sheltered.

2004 +30%

'In many ways for a DVD (defensive value plus dividends) investor like myself 2004 has been a classic year with very little on the downside, profitable corporate activity, many growth stories, and a good continuing flow of dividends.'

Takeovers of niche broker and property financier Wintrust by Singer & Friedlander; Headway, an owner of small industrial estates, by Jack Petchey; and an MBO at property company Estates & Agency. Property star Town Centre has quintrupled in six years!

2005 +20%

Four takeovers this year – departmental store chain James Beattie, banker/lender Broadcastle, Countryside Properties and RAC. A good year for property developer/construction services Pochin's – up 50%, with publisher Quarto entering my portfolio for the first time. Out went aerosols/cosmetics supplier Swallowfield after a 'Christmas nasty' with another profits warning and a passing of its interim dividend. 'Swallowfield has become a serial disappointer and I incurred a painful loss. I am now resolved to adopt a much tougher approach to my laggards. There are plenty of excellent stocks to invest in – my portfolio is not a joint venture with the Salvation Army!'

2006 +18%

'The final year of my relationship with my 40% sleeping partner, Gordon Brown, has delivered 18% capital growth and therefore he will be receiving a very handsome farewell capital gains tax cheque later this month.'

Another good year for takeovers: Welsh microbiologist Biotrace, spotted early in the year and purchased 13 times between 87p and 97.5p, succumbed to a 130p cash bid from 3M, and garden centre Wyevale went to Scottish entrepreneur Tom Hunter – both PEP/ISA tax sheltered. However, bids for Alternative Investment Market (AIM)-quoted electrical products GET and caravan parks operator Parkdean will trigger future capital gains tax (CGT) bills. Thankfully only one modest negative in 2006 – environmental services Fountains, where I bailed out on the loss of confidence in its management.

2007 –14%

'To say that 2007 was an interesting investment year would be an understatement ... the cooler subprime winds were already beginning to be felt on this side of the Atlantic.'

Although palm oil MP Evans, soaps/toiletries PZ Cussons and Irish/UK drugs distributor United Drug hit new highs, and house-builder Ben Bailey was taken over, these bright spots were heavily outweighed by heavy falls in Pochin's, leisure industry services Christie Group, software specialist Delcam, and window ventilation Titon.

2008 –42%

Unquestionably my worst ever year! I wrote: '"The people of England are never so happy as when you tell them they are ruined," quipped Arthur Murphy, the eighteenth-century actor and dramatist. But I doubt it is the sentiment of today's private investor, who approaches 2009 with a ravaged portfolio. We are all in uncharted territory. Nobody knows whether recession will merge into depression; my gut instinct is that we will muddle through and avoid an "Armageddon" scenario ... most "proper" businesses are undervalued by any normal yardstick. There has to be a closing of the gap between dividend yields and the minimal returns on cash deposits.'

I ended my 2008 summary article by forecasting: 'History should show that 2009 represented a great buying opportunity.'

2009 +28%

This year saw me benefiting from a strong recovery in the markets, with virtually all my holdings showing gains. Indeed, I felt that some shares had over-recovered and thus I took profits. Building products supplier Marshalls, which I had bought at 66p last December, were sold for 132p; similarly, three-quarters of my Leeds-based Town Centre Securities that I had bought in February at 60p went out at 182p – an extraordinary trebling in seven months. Two new AIM purchases – Concurrent Technologies and Pressure Technologies – did well, and I doubled my holding in London pub chain Capital Pub, which looked very good value.

2010 +29%

Another good year. Pride of place goes to electro-optical/laser specialist Gooch & Housego with a trebled share price, closely followed by conveyor belting specialist Fenner, which doubled; 11 other holdings appreciated 50% or more. On the debit side, a loss on BP, a further drift in Pochin's and a farewell to HMV, an unnecessary and unfortunate speculation which I got plain wrong! Only one takeover this year, of equity release specialist Sovereign Reversions, by the much larger property group Grainger.

2011 –2%

A disappointing and difficult year. If I take into account dividends of around 3.5% then I am probably just in positive territory in terms of overall return, but that is scant consolation for all my efforts. It was a year of mixed fortunes. On the positive side, three good takeovers – Smiths News for the rump of Dawson Holdings, Greene King, very profitably for Capital Pub, and American insurance broker AmWINS for THB. Also a good realised profit on defence/engineering MS International, bought two years ago at 115p, sold just shy of £3. On the negatives, my 'dog' has been Cable & Wireless Worldwide, down 75%. New purchases included newspaper/periodicals distributor Smiths News on a near 10% yield and price earnings ratio (PER) of 5! It has proved a great 'buy'.

2012 +24%

After a negative 2011, back on track with a solidly profitable year. I have added to three holdings after initial meetings with their CEOs: leading air charter broker Air Partner, natural feeding additives for animals Anpario, and insurance services Charles Taylor. I finally lost patience with window ventilation specialist Titon, taking a loss, as I also did on Cable & Wireless Worldwide following its takeover by Vodafone. However, these two realisations gave me the funds for the aforementioned purchases. Software specialist Delcam is now really starting to motor, forecasting 2012 results 'ahead of market expectations'. It is a classic example of many of my 'long fuse' holdings, where I buy for the long term, patiently waiting for profits growth and, hopefully, an upwards re-rating, and then witnessing and enjoying an 'explosion' in their share prices.

My 12 guiding principles to making a million slowly

These are the rules or principles that I've followed over the past 50 years of investing. I'll talk about them in more detail as I go through the book, but taken as a whole, these provide some key lessons for the investor.

1 Endeavour to buy shares on modest valuations – hopefully with an attractive yield and single-figure price earnings ratio and/or discount to net asset value/real worth.

2 Ignore the overall level of the stock market. Don't make judgements on the macro outlook – leave that to commentators and economists. Focus on your particular selection.

3 Be prepared to hold for a minimum of five years.

4 Have a broad understanding of the PLC's main business activity – one which makes sense to you.

5 Ignore minor share price movements. Looking back years hence you will have got it either right or wrong; whether you originally paid, say, 55 pence rather than 50 pence will be totally irrelevant.

6 Seek established companies with a record of profitability and dividend payments – avoid start-ups and biotech or exploration stocks.

7   Look for moderately optimistic or better chairman's/CEO's most recent comments.

8   Focus on preferably conservative, cash-rich companies or those with low levels of debt.

9   Ensure the directors have meaningful shareholdings themselves in the PLC and 'clean' reputations.

10 Look for a stable Board – infrequent directorate changes. Similarly with professional advisers.

11 Face up to poor decisions. Apply a 20% 'stop-loss' – sell and move on. However, ignore stop-loss if there is a major overall market fall.

12 Let profitable holdings run. Don't try to be too clever, i.e. selling and hoping the market will fall to 'buy back' at a lower price.

Early days: a brief personal journey

was born in 1942 to a general practitioner father and a child psychologist mother, growing up in the Manchester suburb of Davyhulme. We lived above and alongside my father's surgery and I remember padding across the road to our local post office to buy National Savings stamps, using pocket money augmented by pennies from occasionally helping out with a milk delivery round – the start of my capitalist journey. When I was 12 we moved to a larger house and here I first became aware of something called 'the stock market'.

My father had taken over one of the larger downstairs rooms for his library/office and I remember him sitting rather uncomfortably on the floor, pipe in mouth, wading through voluminous piles of the now defunct *Stock Exchange Gazette* and the still published *Investors Chronicle*.

Initially I used to joke about his investment activities – a big hobby. Like many GPs I think he had a sneaking feeling that had he gone into business or the financial world, he would have been quite successful, and the stock market also gave him an opportunity to build up his savings.

As I grew older I started to delve into these mysterious weekly periodicals myself. Dad also signed up for the *IC (Investors Chronicle) Newsletter* and a printed 'Tip-sheet' produced by someone called Beveridge, who used to recommend BET, Land Securities, Great Portland Estates, etc.

My first investment

In the 1950s there were numerous quoted shipping companies and at the age of 15 I selected one called Aviation & Shipping for my first ever investment – heaven knows why – costing all of £45. I remember proudly clutching my first contract note from my father's brokers, a two-partner Mancunian firm called Stothard Brockbank. Suffice to say this purchase was a total disaster – its one ship sank, taking my holding with it! The reverse of beginner's luck, but thankfully I persevered.

Unfortunately my first investment ledger disappeared years ago and thus I have no recollection and record of my immediate following purchases. Interestingly though, I still have a brown booklet from October 1960 issued to clients by Stothard Brockbank, containing statistics on all quoted stocks – it makes fascinating reading. No less than 43 'Breweries and Distilleries' from majors like Distillers, then capitalised at £300 million, Ind Coope, Watneys and Whitbread, to tiddlers such as Bents, Friary Meux, Newcastle, Threlfall's and Yates Castle. Over time this sector has seen merger on merger until today we have only a handful of quoted breweries to invest in. In fact, this is the main message from the booklet: just how few of the then quoted companies have survived today as separate entities – Imperial Tobacco, Rolls-Royce, Unilever, and one or two others being the exceptions. Birmingham Small Arms, Blackpool Tower, Metal Box, Park Cake Bakeries, Shiloh Spinners, Smiths Potato Crisps, Steel Company of Wales, Vickers and dozens of others have mostly been subsumed over the years, and some have gone under.

The trend towards globalisation and economies of scale has seen many companies subsumed. Many readers will still probably bear the scars of the Marconi debacle – a great company brought down by a disastrous American acquisition. But how wonderful to see in 1960 36 'Tea, Coffee and Rubber' companies to invest in – Singlo Tea yielding 24% and New Crocodile River Rubber a more modest 13%. Sadly, all have disappeared.

In 1959, following a two-day visit to the London-based Institute of Industrial Psychology, at which they recommended accountancy as a career for me, I left William Hulme's Grammar School to join the medium-sized Mancunian chartered accountancy firm of Royce Peeling Green, a 17-year-old articled clerk on £4 a week – but my first foot on the commercial ladder.

I started keeping my first black investment ledger. In it I recorded all my transactions from 1963 onwards. It is vital to keep a record of all your transactions, for obvious reasons, and also for capital gains calculations for tax returns. Instructing a broker to sell a holding of shares greater than you actually own can be an embarrassing and potentially expensive mistake to put right.

❝ it is vital to keep a record of all your transactions, for obvious reasons ❞

On 4 December 1963 I bought 500 Sungei Bahru Rubber Estates (it might have been a Beveridge recommendation) at 2s.2d for a total cost of £55.3s.10d (£975 in today's money), and then another 500 in 1964 at a cost of £55.19s.6d. The 1,000 were sold in January 1966 for £83.18s.1d – a sadly recorded loss on sale of £27.5s.3d. Things were looking up – only a partial, not a total, loss!

However, in 1964 it appears that I broke into profit – £1.5s.2d on a holding of W. G. Allen (Tipton) Ltd. Next in 1965 losses on maker of Beaufort life rafts Frankenstein Group, and housebuilders Howarth of Burnley, before a good run of profits – on plastics products Sharna Ware £22.17s.1d; £10.2s.1d on mudguard manufacturer Robert R. Stockfis; £1.3s.11d on textiles Sir T. and A. Wardle; and £9.15s.9d on pillows/duvets E. Fogarty. Hopefully I was beginning to get my eye in, becoming increasingly engrossed in the world of city columns and annual reports.

These days company annual reports can be huge documents, full of detailed information, much of which is of limited interest to the average investor. However, do focus on directors' shareholdings – any changes compared with last year, the level of borrowings and particularly the comments of the chairman and the CEO on future prospects. A comment such as 'We are now well placed to benefit from any improvement in the world economy' usually means don't expect much improvement in the short term. However, comments like 'current order intake and profitability are running well ahead of last year' are much more encouraging.

My career

By 1964 I had qualified as a chartered accountant and moved on to the leading Manchester stockbroking firm of Henry Cooke Lumsden, soon becoming PA to the senior partner, David Hunter. He was a great ambassador, leader and delegator of absolute integrity. It was a privilege, many years later, to be asked by his family to speak at his funeral. I remember referring to him as one of the North West's 'Tall Trees' – for that is what he was. HCL, subsequently absorbed by Brown Shipley, remains my main broker to this day. They give me an excellent personal service. I thoroughly enjoyed my time with them, learning a lot, but after two years I felt the urge to try to create something of my own.

❝ after two years I felt the urge to try to create something of my own ❞

I left to form Second City Securities, an agency company specialising in amalgamations and mergers, which developed into a small investment banking group. With colleagues we bought the controlling interest in a quoted investment trust, Kniton, injected Second City into it, then returned to the stock market and made two successful takeovers of quoted companies – ship repairers the Manchester Dry Docks Company and then mechanical services Ellis (Kensington). Both of these were 'assets' situations, which effectively gave us the capital to start our own bank, Chancery Trust, in the early 1970s.

Following a major medical operation in 1972 I sold my holding as the world of politics beckoned. This provided a modest capital base and the resource to expand my stock market activities. I was adopted as Conservative candidate for Manchester Moss Side, a 'safe' inner-city Labour seat in 1974, fighting the October election unsuccessfully. However, I thoroughly enjoyed the experience, going on to win selection as candidate for marginal Nelson and Colne in Lancashire in 1975. Parallel to all this

I was invited to join Paterson Zochonis PLC, described then as an 'overseas trader', to help them expand their soaps/toiletries/cosmetics interests by taking over Cussons, also Manchester-based. Suffice to say that after a brief takeover battle we prevailed, creating Paterson Zochonis Cussons. PZC, as it is known today, has arguably become one of the North West's greatest post-war commercial successes. I first invested in 1976 – today it is one of my largest shareholdings, and I refer to it on many occasions later in this book.

In the 1979 general election I became a Member of Parliament – the first Thatcher 'gain' of the night, retaining the enlarged and renamed Lancashire constituency of Pendle in 1983 and again in 1987, before being defeated as expected in 1992, primarily on the poll tax disaster. In 1981 I became Parliamentary Private Secretary to my good friend Kenneth (now Lord) Baker, then Information Technology Minister. From 1983 to 1986 I was appointed Under Secretary of State (Defence Procurement) at the Ministry of Defence serving under Michael (Lord) Heseltine and then – post the Westland saga – George (Viscount) Younger. From 1987 to 1989 I held a similar post at the Department of Employment under both David (Lord) Young and then Norman (Lord) Fowler. From 1987 to 1989 I also was Minister of Tourism. Following my election defeat I stayed away from politics, finally resigning from the Conservative Party in 1997 as it became, in my view, increasingly anti-European and more right-wing.

Out of politics, I did three terms as chairman of the Museum of Science and Industry in Manchester and two as chairman of the Christie Hospital NHS Trust, the North West's leading cancer treatment centre. I also served for ten years as a non-executive director of PZC, for a number of years as a trustee of the Refuge Assurance Pension Fund, and for a year in 1998 was appointed High Sheriff of Greater Manchester. In 1990 I was appointed chairman of the Association of Leading Visitor Attractions, the trade body representing those national attractions receiving more than 1 million visitors per annum – the British Museum, Blackpool Pleasure Beach, the Tate, the V&A, Westminster Abbey, etc. Today – 2013 – we have 50 members.

Other former non-executive directorships have included public companies James Halstead, James R. Knowles and M. S. International, and currently I am on the Board of successful private property company Emerson (Developments) Holdings Ltd and Wellington Market Group, quoted on the ICAP Securities & Derivatives Exchange (ISDX).

> **"through all these years my stock market activities have been my great hobby "**

Having joined the Liberal Democrats I was appointed a 'working peer' by the then leader, Charles Kennedy. I was 'introduced' to the House of Lords in 2006.

Through all these years my stock market activities have been my great hobby.

Valuations

What I look for

I have always believed that most investors and analysts over-complicate matters. I try to focus on just two yardsticks when investing in a trading company, e.g. PZ Cussons: dividend yields and PERs, and two for an investment or property company, e.g. Daejan – net asset values (NAVs) and gearing, i.e. the level of borrowings a company has relative to assets. The gearing factor importantly also applies to trading companies.

Dividend yield

Company A has a share capital of £1,000 in shares of £1 each.

It pays a dividend of 10p on every share.

Thus, if an investor buys £100 worth of shares at £1 each they will receive a dividend of 100 × 10p = £10.

Therefore their return is £10 on an investment of £100, i.e. they have bought on a 10% yield.

However, if the share price has risen to £2:

The investor's £100 will buy only 50 shares.

Thus their dividend will be only 10p × 50 = £5.

Therefore they have bought on a 5% yield (£5 on £100).

Price earnings ratios

PERs work on the same principle.

Company B makes pre-tax profits of:	£1,000
It pays corporation tax of 20%:	£200
Therefore its after-tax profits are:	£800

If the company has a share capital (the total amount of money/investment subscribed for by investors, and thus available for use in the business) of, say, £8,000 divided into 8,000 shares of £1 each, which also have a market price of £1, then the price earnings ratio is the total market capitalisation, i.e. £8,000 (8,000 × £1).

Divided by the post-tax profits as above, £800:

Therefore it stands on a price earnings ratio of 10: £8,000 ÷ £800

However, if the share price rises from £1 to £2, then Company B has a market capitalisation of £16,000 (8,000 × £2).

Its after-tax profits are still £800.

Therefore it is on a price earnings ratio of 20: £16,000 ÷ £800

A single-figure PER indicates that, rightly or wrongly, a company is modestly rated – that there is a limited expectation or uncertainty about further profits growth. Initially, investing on a lowish PER – something I try to do – is 'safer' than buying into a share on a PER of, say, 20+. In the case of the latter, the high PER means that the expectation of profits growth is already built into the share price. Fine, if it does deliver, but if it fails to do so then its rating could 'fall'. Thus if a PER rating on a particular PLC falls from 20 to 10, the shares will have halved – bad news!

Let us put dividends and price earnings ratios together in Example C, shown opposite.

Personally, I like to buy shares on a modest valuation – ideally, say, a dividend yield of 5–6% – and on a single-figure PER. Apart from the obvious attractions of receiving the dividend, the payment of a dividend acts as a significant discipline on the Board of a PLC in that it has to find the cash, each year, to pay those dividends.

Company C has capital of £10,000 divided into 10,000 shares of £1 each.

It makes a pre-tax profit of:	£1,000
Pays tax at 20%:	£200
Therefore profit after tax:	£800
It then pays out in dividends:	£200
Retained profits:	£600

(We say the dividend is covered four times by available profits, i.e. £800 ÷ £200)

Company C is capitalised at £10,000.

Its PE ratio is therefore £10,000 ÷ £800 = 12.5

However, if its shares stood at £2, then it would be capitalised at £20,000 and its PE ratio would be £20,000 ÷ £800 = 25 (very expensive).

As far as dividend yield is concerned with the shares at £1:

Let's say the investor owns all Company C's shares, they would receive £200 of dividends on their £10,000 investment.

Their yield would be: $\frac{200}{10,000} \times 100 = 2\%$ (quite modest)

Now what should you look for in the ideal investment? What we want is a company that increases profits (and hopefully dividends) each year and where the rating (PE ratio) that the stock market/ investors place on the company's shares increases significantly. This is the 'double whammy' any investor should be seeking.

Company D makes profits of £100,000.

It has a share capital of £800,000 in £1 shares.

Its shares stand in the market at £1 each.

	£100,000
Less corporation tax 20%	£20,000
Post-tax	£80,000
Stock market capitalisation	
800,000 × £1 =	£800,000

(i.e. it is on a PER of 10: £800,000 ÷ 80,000)

➡

Now let us say profits double to: £200,000

Less 20% corporation tax: £40,000

                                                                             £160,000

And the stock market, because Company D is doing so well and is expected to increase profits again next year, values it not on a PER of 10 but on a PER of 20, so it is capitalised at: 20 × £160,000 = £3.2 million

Therefore each £1 share is now trading at £4 (£3,200,000 ÷ 800,000)

So although profits have only doubled, the shares have quadrupled. A double whammy.

As an investor, that's what you should be looking for: increased profits plus an upward re-rating.

Keeping a record

In April 2000 I wrote about Vimto, a soft drinks manufacturer (see below). This makes the point perfectly.

New fizz from the kings of Vimto

But John Lee discovers that the company has much more to offer these days

For most investors, Nichols Vimto is a rather dour north of England company battling against the might of Pepsi and Coca-Cola.

But it holds many memories for me: not only did I drink Vimto as a schoolboy, it was an early share in my late mother's portfolio. More recently, my investment ledger records a near trebling of the share price between purchase in 1991 and sale in 1995.

A visit to Nichols Vimto's spanking new headquarters, midway between Manchester and Liverpool, gives a very different perspective. John Nichols, executive chairman, and Gary Unsworth, the first non-family managing director, point out that Vimto itself accounts for little more than 25 per cent of turnover. In reality, the group is now a broadly-based beverage company; hence the proposed name change to Nichols plc.

The "new" Nichols produces hot drink systems for Little Chef, Burger King, and British Petroleum. Through its Cabana subsidiary, it is third in the market for supplying draught soft drinks to pubs and clubs. It has also just won its first NHS order: for 20 hot drink trolleys at the Middlesex Hospital.

The group's three former drink manufacturing units have been brought together in a new facility producing Vimto, Sunkist orange and Indigo.

Its fast-growing foods/ingredients business supplies own-brand products for vending machines, and food sachets for the hotel and catering sectors.

The plan is to double food sales over five years. All this reorganisation and change has inevitably led to a plateau in profits, but it points to a very different future.

Nichols has always delivered a progressive dividend. At about 100p, the shares yield around 9 per cent and are bumping along the bottom on a price/earnings ratio of only 6.5. The dividend is twice covered by earnings. For me, it is an ideal stock for personal equity plans or individual savings accounts. I have been buying both before and after the recent results.

My hope is that more investors will recognise the metamorphosis that has transformed Nichols. In December, the group bought back nearly 5 per cent of its equity. It would, almost certainly, have bought more had it not been barred from doing so because of the 60-day close period around the results announcement.

This brings me to an interesting issue: just who is supposed to benefit from the closed period restriction on companies buying their own shares?

The share price invariably sags when the company itself is barred from the market, meaning that sellers get a less attractive price. Conversely, this is a window of opportunity for shrewd prospective buyers who are prepared to study close period dates carefully.

I fully accept the logic of restricting directors' share trading – but why the company? Nichols is clearly frustrated by its lowly stock market value, and I sense a real desire by John Nichols and Gary Unsworth to raise its profile and deliver shareholder value. A new share incentive scheme will certainly focus the minds of key executives.

Source: Lee, J. (2000) New fizz from the kings of Vimto, *Financial Times*, 23 April.

Author note

Nichols has been one of my most successful investments in recent years. The key was the company's decision to 'outsource' production, leaving management to focus on marketing and distribution. In addition, capital was no longer tied up in the manufacturing process. Profits growth and a re-rating have delivered the 'double whammy' which we seek and the shares have appreciated over ten-fold since I wrote this article.

I paid 100p per share on a yield of 9% and on a PER of 6.5 – very modest valuations. Nichols made a crucial decision a few years ago to outsource the production of Vimto and to focus its energies on marketing both in the UK and overseas, particularly in the Gulf States. Profits and dividends have since grown apace and the shares have been substantially re-rated. They are now around £12 each, with a dividend yield of 1.5% and a PER of 28. It has been an outstanding investment and currently is one of my largest holdings.

The article 'Dicing with dividends' overleaf records me being able to pick up Fenner – one of our most successful niche engineering companies in conveyor belting, etc. – after the 2008 financial crisis on a 9% yield at 65p and 70p. Profits growth and a re-rating took them up to nearly £5 before slipping back below £4. Unfortunately I sold half my holding too early at £1.85p, but still at treble those first purchases.

The following article 'Plenty of potential in store' records me buying into department store retailer James Beattie, on a 'double eight' – an 8% dividend yield and a PER of 8. Modest valuations, particularly as it had no gearing (borrowing). However, looking back at my investment records Beattie was not a great success. I paid just over 180p early in 1998, selling later that year at 140p and early in 1999 at 170½p – so an initial loss. Nevertheless, I bought again in 2003–4 at between 113p and 131p, taking a small profit later that year before finally being on the receiving end of a cash takeover in September 2005 at 168p. So not a great success – probably breakeven overall – but as most of the transactions were in my PEPs/ISA, at least I had some much appreciated tax-free dividends.

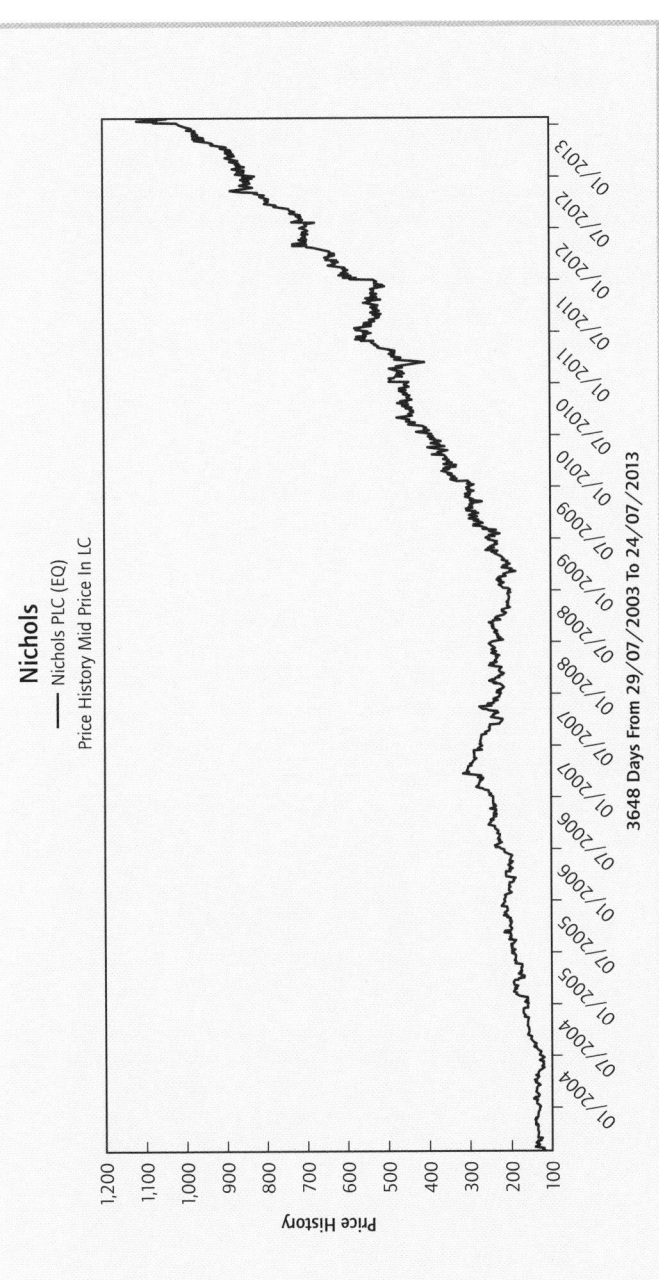

Nichols

— Nichols PLC (EQ)
Price History Mid Price In LC

Price History

3648 Days From 29/07/2003 To 24/07/2013

Note the importance of being patient: although the shares appreciated in those early years, it was 2009 before Nichols really started to motor

Source: Lipper, a Thomson Reuters company

Dicing with dividends

John Lee

When I first started to take an interest in the stock market 50 years ago, the big figure dividend yields were offered mainly by plantation companies – rubber and tea stocks pregnant with nationalisation and commodity risk, or the occasional rather speculative shipping line – sectors that have virtually ceased to exist.

Then I remember the secondary banking/stock market crash of the early 1970s when equities were totally friendless and any number of established plcs offered huge yields. Investors who bought in then did extremely well when markets recovered. Today, we are in an extraordinary period when not only do large caps yield 5–6 per cent and "proper" small caps twice that, but returns on cash deposits are minuscule.

It is thus hardly surprising that we are beginning to see some braver – I would say shrewder – souls edging back into individual savings accounts (Isas). In the last two months, more people were buying than selling Isas for the first time since April 2008. Net inflows in December were treble those of a year ago. Of cource, most investors are still clinging to cash – paralysed with uncertainty and shock at our financial meltdown. But, when recovery and optimism return, sentiment could change very quickly.

Currently, I am very focused on dividends – accepting that few shares are likely to show capital growth in the short term. From my higher-yielding stocks, I am hoping for maintenance of dividends – a dividend increase is a bonus; a "passing" or slashing of the payment is bad news. These board decisions reflect not only the profitablity/debt levels of the company, but also its attitude to shareholder dividends, so past dividend history is an important consideration – as is the size of directors' holdings.

February saw me make two further purchases of Fenner, the conveyor belting/advanced polymer products company on a 9 per cent yield – tax-free within my Isa. Almost a year ago, the company "placed" shares at 223p with institutions to raise funds primarily for a US acquisition. I added to my holding at 65p and 70p – highlighting the ridiculous hammering of word-class businesses such as Fenner. What other class of asset – certainly not house prices or even commercial property – has fallen by anything like this percentage?

Writing in November's annual report, the company's financial director said: "The group is well placed, not withstanding the current disruption of financial markets, to fund and support its operations, with continuing access to medium and long-term debt finance, cash resources and, where necessary, shorter-term facilities." The chairman concluded: "Despite the inevitable challenges, we believe we are very strongly placed to outperform. For the longer term, our business drivers remain highly positive." Hardly the language of a likely dividend cut!

Elsewhere, very recent maintained dividends from BBA Aviation (final) and Town Centre (interim) produced modest share price appreciation, as did Bodycote and Vitec's small dividend increases – all with encouraging trading statements. Current yields on all four are still between 7 and 13 per cent.

I couldn't resist picking up more Town Centre at 60p – it was at 64p in 1999 that I first bought into it, selling some shares at 138p in 2002 and more at 595p in 2006. Property shares are hardly flavour of the month but the yield and a NAV of 270p are tempting.

 Source: Lee, J. (2009) Dicing with dividends, *Financial Times*, 7 March.

Author note

Here I am drawing readers' attention to the way stock market movements are often exaggerated both ways – sometimes too bullish, sometimes too bearish. I was convinced that the subprime banking/financial crisis had driven many quality shares down to absurdly low levels. I was delighted, for example, to buy conveyor belting manufacturer Fenner on a 9% yield. Subsequently they rose to nearly £5 before falling back somewhat as the world's mining industry became less buoyant.

Plenty of potential in store

It's in an unloved sector, but John Lee has lots of time for James Beattie

Retailers are out of favour with investors. So perhaps it is understandable that those of us outside the Midlands value the James Beattie department store group on a "double eight" – dividend yield of 8 per cent and price/earnings ratio of eight.

But surely the thousands of customers who shop at Beatties each week must appreciate that the shares are worth more? I recently visited the Solihull store to meet managing director Chris Jones, who has been with the group for 35 years, and finance director Bill Kelly, and was impressed.

I invested in Beatties in 1998, attracted by the yield and cash pile on the balance sheet. As the share price drifted, I became bored and took a loss. After my recent visit I repurchased (at virtually my selling price), but this time I knew far more about the company.

Beatties, founded in 1877, has nine stores, and is described by market reseach company Verdict as "a strong, impressively profitable and enduring player". It sells branded goods to middle-class customers, with a big emphasis on ladies' clothes, fashion accessories, perfumery, and household and leisure goods.

The group has delivered shareholder value, albeit unrecognised in the share price. Since 1996, on the back of operating margins rising from 5.7 per cent to 8.8 per cent, earnings per share have nearly doubled. Dividends have risen 70 per cent. Beatties has always maintained a high payout ratio and is content with a one-and-a-half times dividend cover.

While profits to January, which should be announced early next month, are forecast to plateau, the scale of the group's expansion has yet to be reflected in the shares' rating. The group

James Beattie
Share price (pence)

Source: Thomson Financial Datastream

has set about increasing its selling space by 50 per cent. This is forecast to cost £28m (half the current market capitalisation) and is being financed almost entirely from internal resources. New stores will open in Birmingham this year, in Huddersfield in 2002 and, it is hoped, in Gloucester the following year.

The five-floor Birmingham store in Corporation Street, formerly C&A, is regarded as a coup, and should be profitable from year one.

In many ways Beatties is a textbook exercise: a settled and ambitious management, an emphasis on staff training, low employee turnover, coupled with a ruthless "clean stock" policy and a "customer is always right" attitude.

As an investment it offers yield, nil gearing, full asset backing and every opportunity for a re-rating as profits advance over the next two to three years.

For income seekers there is an 8 per cent yield and scope for steady capital appreciation, spiced with a predatory potential if the shares don't buck up soon.

I also like the board's willingness to build up directors' shareholdings through market purchases, and not just by relying on share options, although these are in place as well.

If I have one criticism, it is that Beatties appears to have put little effort into shareholder relationships. Attendance at the annual meeting is thin, and there are no shareholder discounts or benefits.

 Source: Lee, J. (2000) Plenty of potential in store, *Financial Times*, 24 March.
© The Financial Times Limited 2000. All Rights Reserved.

Author note

My investment in Midlands' department store James Beattie was not a particular success – I probably broke even overall. Its new Birmingham store, once C&A, was not a winner, beset with all sorts of traffic problems. However, the fundamental point here is that because I had bought it at a low level – a dividend yield and a PER both of 8 – there was little downside risk. The key to building an appreciating portfolio is to avoid the losses – don't take unnecessary risks or buy at inflated levels.

Family PLCs

The following article 'Family values at a discount' centres on family-controlled property group Daejan. When I started investing years ago there were quite a number of residential property companies to invest in, but most have been taken over. Daejan represents one of the few opportunities to invest in London residential property today, although it also owns significant commercial property and both residential and commercial property in the USA. With overall gearing of less than 20%, Daejan is an excellent example of a low-risk property investment. In recent years its NAV (assets less liabilities) has been north of £50 per share. My buying has always been at a good discount: between £41.50 in 2007 and £27.10 in 2011. The current price is £40.

Family values at a discount

John Lee

Proprietorial PLCs – companies that are controlled or dominated by one family – have always fascinated me. I hold shares. I like the alignment of board and shareholder interests, the focus on conservative growth and "stewarding" a business through generations, their generally low borrowings and usually progressive dividend policy.

Each has its own characteristics and ethos – and this interests me from a wider sociological perspective. Property company Daejan is a classic example, as I observed when attending its annual general meeting (AGM) last month.

I have held Daejan shares in my individual savings account (Isa) for some time – paying between £29 and £40 in 2007, and then about £27 in 2008 and 2011. In all cases, I was buying at a discount to Daejan's net assets. Today, the share price is £24, capitalising the company at £390m, and the dividend yield is 3 per cent.

Daejan is effectively 80 per cent owned by the Freshwater family, who injected their property interests into a cash "shell" in 1959. Over the years, shareholder returns have been very impressive: since 1981, the share price has appreciated 1,350 per cent and the dividend by 1,950 per cent, having increased annually for the past 30 years. Over a comparable period, the retail prices index has risen by 315 per cent.

About 50 shareholders and advisers attended the AGM, the majority somewhat elderly, for whom the gathering was clearly something of an annual ritual. This audience faced a five-man board – four Freshwaters and one non-executive who dates from 1971 and is thus not regarded as "independent". Daejan's founder, Osias – the father of the present chairman – escaped the Holocaust by leaving Gdansk, Poland, in 1939 on the last vessel out, and arrived in this country virtually penniless. The family commitment to Orthodox Jewry remains very strong and Jewish educational charities have benefited handsomely over the years from the company's generosity.

In the 1960s, the group was the largest private landlord in the UK and, over the years, diversification into commercial property and the US has taken place. At March 31 2011, 80 per cent of the company's £1.25bn-worth of property was in the UK, split between commercial and residential. Daejan is probably the largest residential owner in London.

Overall gearing is low, with borrowings less than 20 per cent. Within the portfolio, the £40m redevelopment of Africa House in Holborn – likely to deliver a £7m annual rent roll – has significant potential.

On the other hand, the portfolio includes nine care homes, leased to Southern Cross, though these are only 2.5 per cent of the total portfolio.

Daejan's annual report discloses a net asset value per share of £51.43p, up from 2010's £48.17p – but even this may be understated.

So, at the current share price, an investor is getting £1 of property for less than 50p. I cannot think of any comparable example.

Daejan is hardly in the vanguard of progressive corporate governance. But the huge discount, participation in London residential values and a hopefully rising 3 per cent dividend yield are compelling. I can also recommend the excellent AGM kosher buffet – many delicacies were reminiscent of my late grandmother's traditional cuisine!

 Source: Lee, J. (2011) Family values at a discount, *Financial Times*, 2 October. © The Financial Times Limited 2011. All Rights Reserved.

Author note

When I wrote this article, property company Daejan's share price was £24 but its net asset value was over £50 – thus it was a 'no-brainer'. Given the company's modest gearing, its shares just had to recover unless we faced a meltdown of Armageddon proportions. I am glad to say that by mid-2013 Daejan's shares had recovered to around £40.

Thus we have two different types of 'value' purchases – Nichols/ Fenner/Beattie on attractive dividend yields and modest PERs, and Daejan at a significant discount to assets.

Value

I must also refer to a third category where the 'worth' of the business is in real terms surely more than the stock market capitalisation. Two examples, Christie, in business services and stocktaking, and Quarto, in book publishing, are in my current portfolio.

Share prices can belie true value

John Lee

My investment approach is based on a belief that "value" always comes through in the end – although I quip that, with some companies, many shareholders will have died waiting! Sometimes it can feel as if I am creating a portfolio for my future grandchildren.

Usually, my investment judgment is based upon relative dividend yields, price/earnings (p/e) ratios, price/earnings growth (PEG) ratios, market expectations, etc. But with property companies, a value assessment is more easily made with professionally certified net asset values – hence my earlier purchases of Daejan and Town Centre at big discounts.

Often, however, there is a clear differential between stock market capitalisation and what a trade buyer or competitor might pay – thus some surprisingly high premiums are seen on takeover bids. I have always felt, for example, that family-controlled flavours/fragrances manufacturer Treatt – my largest holding – is "worth" significantly more than its market capitalisation, although it is determinedly independent.

Occasionally, a glaring anomaly arises particularly with a small PLC that falls below most investors' and analysts' radar: I believe Aim-quoted Christie Group to be a classic example.

I have been "aboard" for 10 years, buying first in the mid-30ps in 2002 and seeing them climb to a peak of 272p when pre-tax profits in double figures were reached.

An expensive software venture then acted as a considerable drag, thankfully now terminated, and trading conditions in recent years have not been easy with dividends passed in 2009/2010.

However, Christie has steadily developed over the years and is highly regarded within its two principal sectors: professional business services, covering valuing, buying, selling, financing a wide variety of businesses in the leisure, care, retail sectors; and stocktaking and inventory systems and services.

Christie's business services are provided from 14 offices in the UK and 13 abroad – having opened in Dubai last year and Dublin very recently – and helped it win Estates Gazette's "Most Active UK Agent" award in the Leisure and Hotels category for a second year. Apart from disclosed clients such as Von Essen Hotels and Southern Cross, it does a substantial amount of work for banks, insurance companies etc, with no publicity. Most of its major competitors are now virtually all overseas-owned.

Christie's stocktaking business – number one in the UK, number three in the world, with 11 offices and more than 1,000 employees – has roots going back to 1846. But new clients include Zara, Butlins, Tesco Pharmacy.

Total group revenue increased to £53m for 2011, split broadly equally between the two divisions. With directors and staff owning 65 per cent, marginal profitability and a recent dividend reduction, the shares have come back to 52p, giving a paltry £13m capitalisation. So I recently added more at 49p to my already sizeable holding. This year has reportedly started well and I expect the high operational gearing to build bottom line profitability.

I would suggest a trade buyer might value Christie at £1 for every pound of turnover – £50m-plus – or four times its present market valuation. But even a more conservative calculation makes a mockery of the present share price. Indeed, the group floated at 145p in 1988, when it was considerably smaller.

Author note

My core investment philosophy is that 'value', i.e. real worth, always comes through in the end, but you must be patient. Here I focus on leisure industry services/stocktaker Christie Group – its share price graph (see figure overleaf) demonstrates wild gyrations over the years. My belief is that any price below £1 represents a bargain; it was 'floated' at 145p in 1988 when the business was much smaller than it is today.

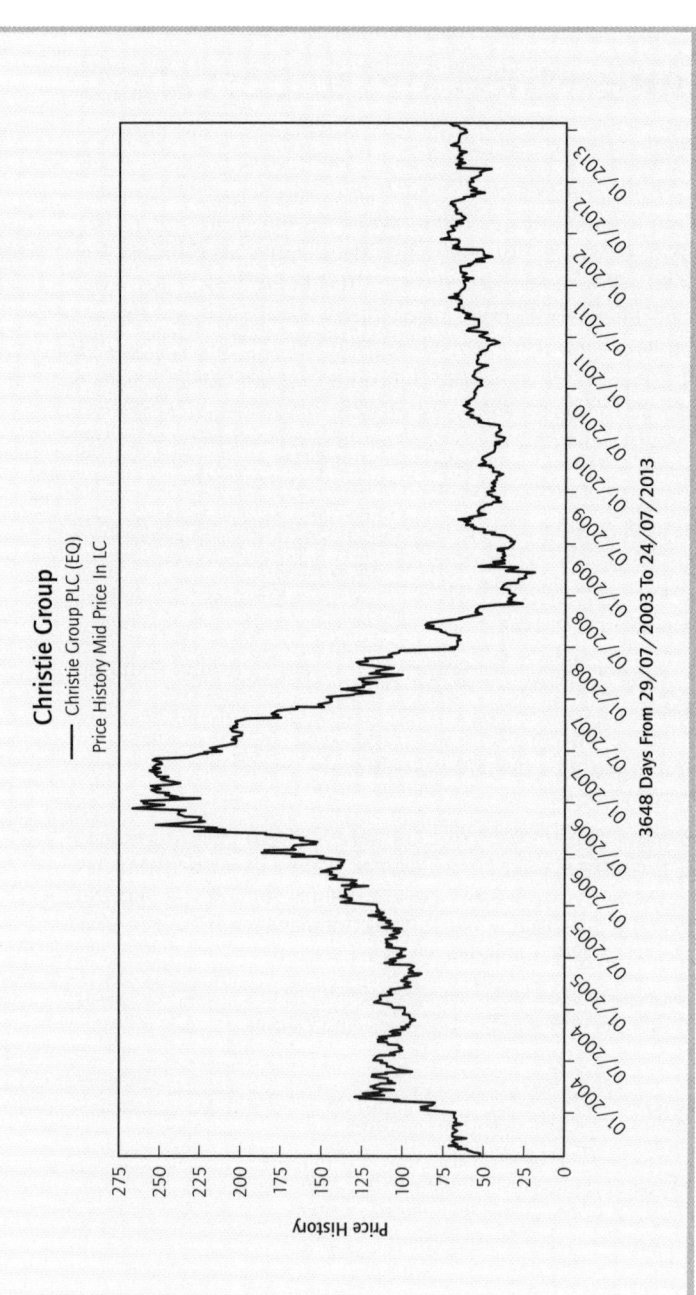

Christie Group
— Christie Group PLC (EQ)
Price History Mid Price In LC

3648 Days From 29/07/2003 To 24/07/2013

They touched nearly 275p in 2006 – now less than one-third of that. Hopefully, in time ...

Source: Lipper, a Thomson Reuters company

Misunderstood and undervalued

John Lee

The most frequent complaint from small-cap chief executives is that their companies are misunderstood and their shares are undervalued. Occasionally, this frustration spills over – as in the case of Laurence Orbach, founder and driving force of Quarto, the international book publisher.

In his chairman's letter accompanying the recent 2010 results, he writes: "I know that it is considered inappropriate for executives and directors of publicly traded companies to stick their necks out and proclaim that their businesses are not understood by investors and should be more highly rated.

"I risk opprobrium for voicing my dismay that Quarto shareholders have not been better served by my explanations of the company's virtues to the investing community. We have grown our business over the years, but could do much more if we were trading on a higher multiple of earnings."

I concur, and happily declare my own interest as a long-standing shareholder.

Over the years, I have made 20 purchases – mainly for my personal equity plan (Pep) and individual savings account (Isa) – at prices between 211p and 88p.

Quarto is one of the largest international co-edition book publishers with two main strands of activity: its publishing segment publishes books, under imprints owned by the group; and its co-edition publishing segment creates books that are licensed to third-party publishers for publication under their own imprints.

Overall, 85 per cent of its total revenues derive from outside the UK. It is focused and risk averse, with a business model honed conservatively over the last 35 years.

Essentially, it publishes books of an enduring interest: "not looking for the next big thing, but the next lasting thing".

Quarto's top five sellers in 2010 give a flavour: *Complete Guide to Writing, 1001 Movies you must see before you die, Anatomica Revised, 1001 Songs you must listen to before you die* and *Art: The Whole Story*. None of these exceeds 1 per cent of group revenues – most sales are made through large arts and craft store chains and home improvement retailers.

Recent results showed encouraging profits growth, debt reduction and a welcome 5 per cent dividend increase – with current trading described as "interesting and exciting".

But Quarto's real value is in its niche business model and its £30m backlist of titles from which it derives substantial royalties – its books are sold in 35 countries and 25 languages. At 155p, a price/earnings (p/e) of 6 surely seriously undervalues this £31m capitalised business – offering a 5 per cent dividend yield covered 3.5 times.

Elsewhere, markets have inevitably been unsettled by the Arabic uprisings and consequent rise in the price of oil, but thankfully the majority of announcements emanating from my holdings have been positive.

There have been dividend increases from THB, Town Centre, and Wynnstay, and encouraging statements and newsflow from Capital Pubs, the Cable & Wireless duo, Christie Group, Dairy Crest, Gooch and Housego, MS International, Norcros, Park Group, Primary Health, S+U and United Drug, with "old friend" Dawson Holdings seemingly engaged in takeover talks.

Author note

'Misunderstood and undervalued' is how I describe book publisher Quarto, a holding which I believe will 'deliver' in the future. The founder and then CEO Laurence Orbach vents his frustration in the annual report: 'I risk opprobrium for voicing my dismay that Quarto shareholders have not been better served by my explanation of the company's virtues to the investing community.' Sadly, this brave and honest statement failed to bring about any improvement in Quarto share price and Laurence was deposed by shareholders' vote in 2012. We hope that the new top team will succeed where Laurence unfortunately failed. Public company life can be cruel.

I have held both for many years, confident that in time 'value' will be reflected in either an upward re-rating or a takeover. 'Value' always comes through in the end, but sadly some share-holders may die waiting.

After 50 years of investing it is hardly surprising that I know what characteristics I look for in PLCs that I consider investing in, and the types of shares that I feel comfortable holding long term. Smaller caps, established, profitable, conservative dividend-paying companies, cash positive, or with low levels of debts are for me, preferably having a recognised 'brand' or unique selling point (USP) and preferably also trading internationally. The FTSE Small Cap Index contains smaller companies outside the FTSE 100 and the FTSE 250 indices. These companies make up about 2% of the UK market.

Generally speaking, small caps tend to be less well covered by analysts and thus offer greater opportunities to be 'discovered' by private investors. For me, no small cap can be too small – indeed, approximately 25% of my current portfolio is made up of companies with a market capitalisation of less than £50 million and others were below that figure when I first bought into them. Frequently these are what I term 'family' or 'proprietorial' companies, with control passing through the generations where the emphasis is on 'stewardship', one of my favourite investment words. By this I mean that we usually have family Board members, conscious of the efforts of earlier generations who created and developed the business, and conscious also of their responsibility to add worth and value

❝ for me, no small cap can be too small ❞

during their tenure in a conservative way. So, ideally, organic growth with perhaps an acquisition from time to time, but no excessive risk taking or 'betting the shop' on a large, over-reaching deal.

In addition, those in an executive role often find that there are widows, maiden aunts, siblings or other relatives with significant shareholdings, who are totally reliant on the dividends from the 'family' PLC for their lifestyle. There used to be the saying 'clogs to clogs in three generations' – particularly applicable to many old mill-owning families – but as a generalisation those days are thankfully long gone. The current generation of family PLCs has hopefully recognised that to pass the reins to a member of the family who is just not up to it is a recipe for disaster.

These days one usually finds that a successful Board has a judicious mix of family and 'outsiders', promoted or brought in for their professional abilities rather than the size of their share-holdings. Over the years I have profited greatly from investing alongside families, albeit with far more modest holdings. It was in the 1970s that I started to focus on such companies by buying into the three Ps – Pifco, Pochin's and Paterson Zochonis (now PZ Cussons) – all based in my North West homeland.

Unloved, unwanted and undervalued

Even so, John Lee believes that Pifco has a bright future in the electrical appliances market

For all the interest the stock market takes, Pifco, which makes small electrical appliances, might as well have stayed private under its original name: the Provincial Incandescent Fittings Company.

In spite of having a progressive record and owning valuable consumer brands (including Russell Hobbs, Carmen, Tower, Mountain Breeze and Salton), the company has been ignored by investors. In part, this comes from its profile which stems, I believe, from Michael Webber, chairman and chief executive. He is a very private person as well as a diligent manager.

While having a laudable and comprehensive mission statement, I am not convinced that Pifco has really tried to embrace shareholders. The AGM is held off-site and, although I have been a shareholder since 1977 and have had regular discussions, it was only very recently that I was allowed to cross the drawbridge and enter Fort Pifco – a large, red-brick, former textile mill in the Failsworth district of Manchester.

Pifco is one of several "proprietorial" plcs (my term) where a family either has the controlling shareholding or operates under some similar arrangement. (To its credit, Pifco enfranchised its "A" non-voting shares in 1998).

Succeeding generations regard themselves as stewards, conscious not only of responsibilities to employees, customers and shareholders but also to safeguard the family silver. With luck, they will provide growing dividends income and capital worth for members of the family not active in the business and, often, for charitable trusts and settlements.

Such companies usually are characterised by low borrowings, steady organic growth, modest bolt-on acquisitions and conservative image.

Pifco has much to commend it. It is a tightly managed and cash generative company with new products coming on stream continually. It also has some flexibility of manufacture, either at Wolverhampton or in east Asia, and racked up a very creditable achievement in turning round the loss-making Russell Hobbs in short order. Moreover, it has wasted no time in integrating Hi Tech Industries, a maker of lighting products, which it acquired recently.

How successful it will be in bringing home a bigger acquisition is uncertain. In my view, Pifco needs either to get bigger or be absorbed by a larger international group. It is known to have been circling Kenwood for some time.

Interim results just announced show further progress: pre-tax profits up 12 per cent and the dividend (I criticised the company in an earlier article for being too parsimonious) up 10 per cent and covered three times. Analysts project £4.2m pre-tax profits for the full year to April 30. With the share price around 135p, this implies a miserly price-earnings ratio of seven on a low tax charge.

I found Webber and James Wallace, a key colleague who also has a sizeable shareholding, welcoming and frank. But both had a bad dose of the "triple U" virus – unloved, unwanted and undervalued – that strikes so many smaller company directors today.

Pifco is clearly worth much more than its £24m capitalisation. I would be fascinated to hear just what value a brand consultant would place on it. There is also a large cash pile likely to be around £12m by year-end.

I left with two things. First, I now own a state-of-the-art Russell Hobbs kettle (which will be recorded in the register of shareholders' interests).

Second, I have a clear belief that the Webber/Wallace duo is determined to deliver shareholder value. I would be surprised and disappointed if, in two years, my Pifco holding had not appreciated enough for me to re-equip my whole kitchen.

 Source: Lee, J. (2000) Unloved, unwanted and undervalued, *Financial Times*, 25 March.

Author note

There is a saying that 'small cap' stocks are valued correctly only twice – on original flotation when they first went public, and when they are ultimately taken over. This article refers to electrical appliance manufacturer Pifco, which was my first PEPs purchase. It became one of my favourite holdings – tightly run, cash rich, with valuable brands like Russell Hobbs. Finally it was taken over, very profitably for me, by Salton of the USA in 2001.

Pifco ('Unloved, unwanted and undervalued') was a manufacturer of small electrical appliances – hairdryers, kettles – acquiring Russell Hobbs as it grew. They ran a very tight ship, operating from an old converted mill and always maintaining a large cash pile. Pifco was my first ever PEPs holding. Like PZC, it then had Ordinary and 'A' non-voting shares – as both companies were family controlled, whether I held voting or non-voting shares was somewhat academic, though obviously the 'A' shares were cheaper. Ultimately, with no family succession, Pifco was taken over by Salton in 2001, delivering me a significant profit.

Construction services/property developer Pochin's was originally a great success story. I was impressed with its reputation as a 'quality' builder of schools, offices, warehouses, etc., with its own property developments becoming increasingly important and profitable. My £15,000 investment grew steadily until it was worth over £1 million by 2007. Fortunately, concerned that the share price of nearly £4 was too 'toppy', I sold some of my shares between 367p and 399p – quadrupling my original investment. Then, sadly, near-disaster struck: over-stretched in property development joint ventures, with sizeable borrowings and expensive guarantees, the 2007–8 banking/property crash nearly capsized the company. Thankfully, it survived, but as a shadow of its former self, with the shares currently limping along around 30p or at $\frac{1}{13}$th of their former peak.

" nothing is certain in stock market investing – equity investment always involves a degree of risk **"**

Nothing is certain in stock market investing – equity investment always involves a degree of risk.

Sparring over dividends

From: John Lee, M.P.

HOUSE OF COMMONS
LONDON SW1A 0AA

16th November 1981

A.C. Pochin, Esq.,
Chairman,
Pochin's Limited,
Brooks Lane,
Middlewich,
Cheshire CW10 0JQ

Dear Mr. Pochin,

I write both to congratulate you and the Board on first class results but also to register a considerable degree of irritation and disappointment at the lack of any increase in dividend. I really would have thought that over the last couple of years, during which period the company's growth has continued, culminating in extremely strong assets, liquidity and dividend cover, a modest increase in the dividend would have been the very least that could have been expected. The likely reduction in profits next year would seemingly make it illogical to increase the dividend in that year thus dividends would appear to be marking time for a number of years and in my view, this is unsatisfactory and unfair to certain shareholders.

I speak for family and associated shareholders who own approximately 4% of Pochin's equity - some of whom are smaller shareholders to whom dividend income is important. No doubt there will be many other smaller shareholders in this position who will perhaps also suffer from capital financial loss should they sell their shares on the lower rating which I believe partly follows from restricted dividend policy. It is all very well building up the capital strength of the company, taking the longer view but surely shareholders are entitled to some benefits along the way?

It may well be of course that dividends are rather unimportant to the controlling shareholders and trusts etc. but then surely if this is so, then there is a case for certain shareholders to consider waiving their dividend entitlements, thus perserving the company's liquidity position.

I would have thought that the company's deserved reputation and standing would not have brought the Board to the verge of abusing its position of trust relative to the minority shareholders but I believe that it is in danger of doing this. Should Parliamentary duties permit, I have every intention of coming to the A.G.M. and expressing my views at the meeting. In the meantime, I would be grateful for your comments.

Kind regards.

Yours sincerely,

John Lee, Esq., M.P.

POCHIN'S
Limited

Registered Office
Brooks Lane Middlewich
Cheshire CW10 OJQ
Tel 060-684 3333
Telex 668603
Reg in England No 300573
VAT Reg No 279434227

ACP/GJJ.

24th November, 1981.

2 5 NOV 1981

John Lee M.P.
The House of Commons,
LONDON, S.W.1

Dear Mr. Lee,

I have your letter expressing your congratulations of Pochin's Annual
Accounts and results to May 31st 1981 along with your disappointment
with the Dividend proposals of the Board.

As you are aware even before and during your interest in the Company
of some 5 years or more, we have always had a cautious approach to the
Company's standing and solidarity which may reflect in todays financial
position and share value.

As everyone, and yourself even more so, are fully aware of the many
difficulties Industry is facing at the present time, such as wage
increases, inflation, PAYE and an imposed rate levy (without any referendum),
Industrial Tribunal costs, Insurance levy and the difficulty of obtaining
Contracts at realistic prices etc. that this should bear heavily on the
Board's decision not to increase the Dividend this time, as we wish to be
strong to ride the present difficult period. Your Board have made every
effort to streamline the Company's operations, to reduce waste, increase
discipline and keep the non-producing staff to a minimum by avoiding replacing
natural wastage and early retirement. All the Directors and Senior Staff
are putting in a large amount of time above their normal working day in the
common interest of the Company.

I note your remarks with regard to the waive of Shareholders who hold substantial equity and just for your information, in case you are not aware of
it, that this has been the practice in the past to no small tune by Senior
Board Directors, having waived something in the region of £58,000 between
1971-79. I think you must agree that they should have some entitlement to
the full declared Dividends each year before we increase them any further.

You are no doubt aware that in the Building and Construction Industry the
effect of a recession takes about 18 months and likewise the climb back
takes equally as long, or possibly some 2 years. It is very difficult
to forecast in the future, when even the Government can give no early
prediction and admit that it has taken longer than they anticipated. This
once again is the reason for our cautious approach.

/Continued.....

A C Pochin (Chairman) W R Verity (Managing) M A Pochin N J Pochin MA (Oxon) Mrs S E Nicholson J H Woodcock

Continuation......

The question of whether Company Shares are high or low seems only relative if one wishes to buy or sell Shares, and so long as the performance of the Company is good we feel it better that we should give priority to maintaining this state of affairs. However, with todays value of Shares it would seem quite a good performance for Investors that have been holding the Shares over the last few years.

We shall be pleased to see you, if this is possible, at the Meeting and no doubt you will meet most of the Board if you wish to discuss matters further.

Kind regards.

Yours sincerely,

A.C. Pochin

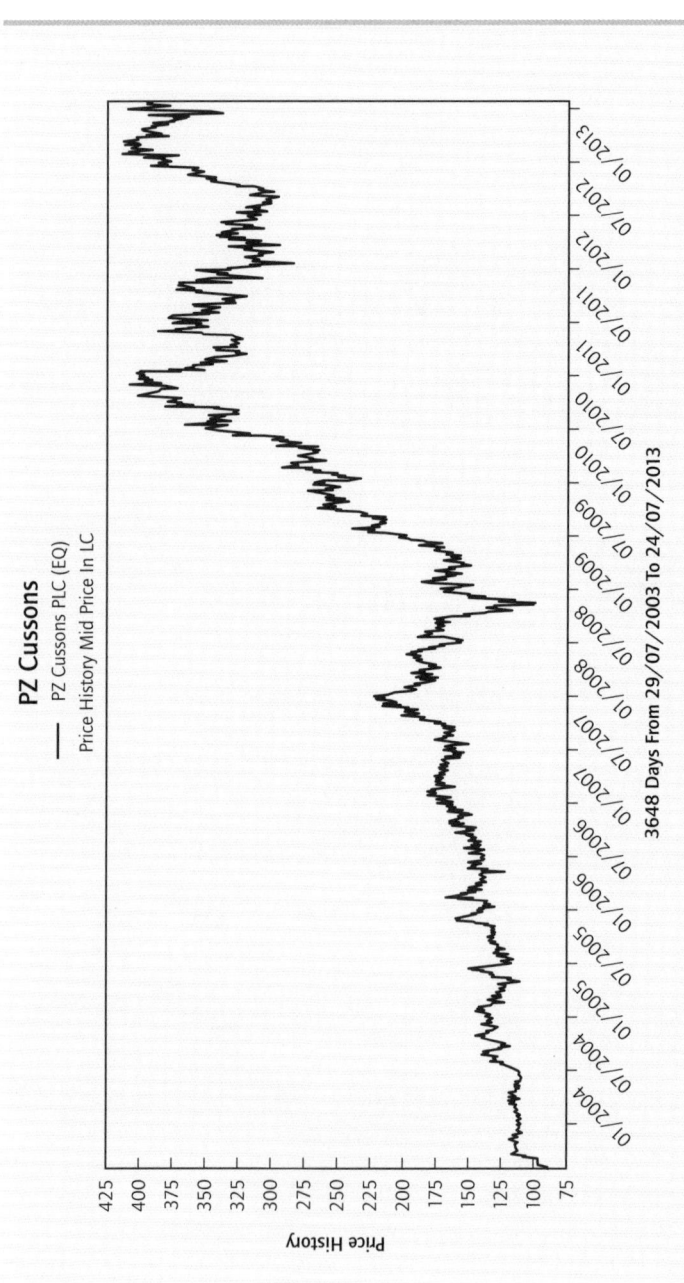

PZ Cussons

— PZ Cussons PLC (EQ)
Price History Mid Price In LC

3648 Days From 29/07/2003 To 24/07/2013

Source: Lipper, a Thomson Reuters company

Just a great success story, but here again patience was required before the upward re-rating took place between 2009 and 2011

PZ Cussons was originally founded by Paterson, a Scot, and Zochonis, a Greek, in the 19th century to export textiles and basic commodities from the UK to Nigeria. Now controlled by the wider Zochonis family, PZC has become a major international manufacturer of soaps, detergents, cosmetics, etc., with substantial operations, particularly in Indonesia, Nigeria and the UK (I declared an interest having been an employee and non-executive director earlier). When PZC went public in the 1950s it was capitalised at just over £1 million; today's capitalisation of £1.7 billion represents spectacular long-term growth, with shareholders not having to put in any further capital. I have been a happy holder for 36 years – today it is one of my largest holdings, with an annual dividend return of approximately 38% on original cost. This is what long-term investment is all about.

Shareholder stamina for a long haul

John Lee

At a time of considerable short-term uncertainty, it is perhaps apposite to remember what serious long-term equity investment is about, and the rich rewards if one chooses well and stays aboard. In 1953, West African merchants Paterson Zochonis went public with a stock market capitalisation of £1.2m. Its £10m annual turnover was thus described by the Evening Standard: "It bought palm oil, cocoa and ground nuts from the natives and sold them everything from combs to motorcars in return". Hardly the politically correct prospectus language of today.

Over the next half century, through many economic cycles and civil war in Nigeria, it has grown into a international manufacturer of brand-based products predominately in the soaps, toiletries, cosmetics and detergents sectors in Europe, Asia and Africa – Nigeria always having been a very important market. Today PZ Cussons, as it is now known, has a turnover approaching £600m, 10,000 employees, with recent interim results indicating likely annual pre-tax profits in the £75m region.

Shareholders have done handsomely with regular annual dividend increases and no financial calls ever having been made on them. The group is now capitalised at £800m – in spite of slipping from its recent ➡

peak. So, anyone who modestly invested in 1953 would be very wealthy today. Sadly, I was only 11 at that time and had not quite started my investing career.

I first invested in PZC in 1976 – it now constitutes one of my largest core holdings. This family-controlled plc has to be one of Manchester's greatest commercial success stories and the city and the North West have benefited greatly from the family's beneficence as 11.5 per cent of the equity is in a charitable trust generating substantial dividend income. An indirect way of investing in PZC is through the £50m capitalised Manchester and London Investment Trust which owns approaching 5m shares, equivalent to 17 per cent of the trust's current worth. This niche trust has been built up successfully by former Manchester stock-broker, Brian Sheppard, and offers one of the UK's most valuable, but largely unknown, shareholder perks. It owns two Wimbledon debentures carrying the annual entitlement to 23 pairs of tickets for the Centre and No.1 Courts during Wimbledon fortnight. To qualify, shareholders must own a minimum of 2,500 shares (approximately £9,000 at current value). A weighted draw is held at the November annual meeting – the Sheppard family and company officers being barred!

For good order, I must place on record that in the past I have been a non-executive director of both PZ Cussons and Manchester and London Investment Trust but claim no credit for both those companies' considerable achievements.

Choosing from the cornucopia of value available in the small cap sector is not easy, but I finally selected shower and tile specialist Norcros as a new purchase last month. Originally having been taken private in 1999, it returned to the stock market – at 78p last year and rose to a peak of 86p. Since then it has been downwards all the way, culminating in nearly 20 per cent of the price being lopped off when it recently announced that profits would be marginally below forecasts. I bought at 42p on a prospective yield next year approaching double figures, following significant directors' buying. Norcros's domestic shower division, brand leader Triton, must itself be worth the entire current group £60m capitalisation leaving its substantial tile interests both here and in South Africa in for free.

Finally, as evidence of the gap between current share prices and reality, just look at builders' merchants, Gibbs and Dandy. In mid-January I bought at 275p. Today, after a takeover approach, they are 390p. I am hoping for a recommended deal well north of £4 – value always comes through in the end.

Source: Lee, J. (2008) Shareholder stamina for a long haul, *Financial Times*, 1 March.

Author note

This 2008 article focuses on PZ Cussons, arguably one of the North West's greatest success stories and one of my major holdings. For years it was misunderstood and largely ignored by investors. In recent years, however, it has achieved the 'double whammy' of profits growth and substantially improved re-rating. Its market capitalisation (share price × number of shares in issue) in 2013 is over twice what it was in 2008.

Greater Manchester can also boast two other golden family stories: international floor coverings manufacturer James Halstead, which has had an outstanding record of year-on-year profits and dividend growth (both my daughters are appreciative shareholders), and in more recent years the aforementioned soft drinks manufacturer Nichols.

I first invested in Nichols in 1991 but only started to build up a worthwhile holding in 2000. What we have seen with Halstead, Nichols and PZC is not only real profits growth but also a significant 're-rating' – moving on to a much higher PE ratio – thus delivering the 'double whammy' which is so beneficial to investors, as I discussed earlier.

Other 'happy family' successes for me include London-based electrical accessories manufacturer (plugs, sockets, light fittings, etc.) GET, taken over by Schneider of France, and three current holdings: short-term Birmingham lender S&U, controlled by the Coombs family; Redditch industrial lighting manufacturer F. W. Thorpe, controlled by the eponymous Thorpe family; and Leeds property investor Town Centre Securities, controlled by the Ziff family. Of course, some family PLCs have been much less successful, but overall this sector has proved a rich seam for me.

> ❝ some commentators regard family control as a negative ... I take the opposite view ❞

Some commentators regard family control as a negative, as they do large dominating directors' shareholdings. I take the opposite view. I want those running my PLC investments to have large holdings – the larger the better – then I know that our interests are truly aligned.

5

Spotting opportunities

Research

How should an aspiring investor get started? Not an easy one to answer, but I suggest you begin by reading the business sections of daily or weekend newspapers, and browse through the range of investment/stock market books available at bookstores or online. Select one or two which appeal.

In my view, to be a successful investor requires commitment and time, and you're only going to put in the required effort if you find the stock market enjoyable and absorbing. To be blunt, either you fall in love with investing – its fascination and its mysteries – or you don't. You will know soon enough which it is. If you don't, there is no shame in this, just forget it – leave the investing of your money to others, either by choosing a mutual fund/ investment or unit trust or giving a stockbroker or bank discretion to handle your portfolio on a mutually agreed basis.

❝ to be a successful investor requires commitment and time ❞

Sources

Assuming now that you enjoy investment articles and investment gossip, then rather more serious research is called for. These days the internet provides a wealth of information on particular quoted companies – all PLCs have a website. Personally, I am still somewhat traditional, preferring the printed word. Apart from the financial columns I regularly subscribe to the weekly *Investors Chronicle*, having done so for many years, and find it an invaluable source of comment and ideas, particularly on the smaller quoted companies on which I focus. They are invariably less well covered by investment analysts and commentators, so the investor has a better chance of unearthing an overlooked 'nugget'. I've been fortunate in doing so on a number of occasions over the years. I also subscribe to *Company REFS* published quarterly (www.companyrefs.co). These give a separate page of information on each quoted company, both main market and AIM, showing, for example, the company's directors, its principal shareholders, its profits and dividend history, and, particularly with larger companies, brokers' estimates of future earnings, etc. See the example on PZ Cussons in the figure opposite.

AIM is a junior market to the main stock exchange market. Its requirements before a company is allowed to 'float' or 'go public' are less demanding than for the main market and costs are lower. Companies quoted on AIM tend to be younger and rather more speculative, but there are still many AIM-quoted companies which are well established and conservatively run. Approaching one half of my holdings are AIM stocks. In some cases, as with Christie and Nichols, they have moved from the main market to AIM to take advantage of a current, very attractive tax break with inheritance tax exemption for most AIM shares provided they have been held for at least two years. AIM shares are now eligible for ISAs, which I, for one, have been campaigning hard for.

approaching one half of my holdings are AIM stocks

The quarterly *Company REFS* pack also has a separate section on 'Directors' Dealings' to which I pay close attention. For me it is crucial that in the companies where I invest the directors themselves have meaningful shareholdings. Sometimes I am horrified – particularly in large cap stocks – that key Board members who are paid substantial sums choose to invest so little in the companies they manage. Of course, many are incentivised by share

394 PZC May 2013 Fully listed companies   Company REFS - Really Essential Financial Statistics

PZ CUSSONS

PRICE (p)   1p Ord vs FTSE All-Share vs norm eps

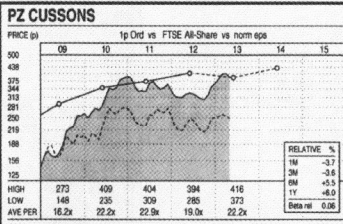

	09	10	11	12	13	14	15
HIGH	273	409	404	394	416		
LOW	148	235	309	285	373		
AVE PER	16.2x	22.2x	22.9x	19.0x	22.2x		

RELATIVE	%
1M	-3.7
3M	-3.6
6M	+5.5
1Y	+6.0
Beta rel	0.06

SECTOR: Personal Goods. **ACTIVITIES:** PZ Cussons PLC is involved in the manufacture & distribution of soaps, detergents, toiletries, beauty products, pharmaceuticals, electrical goods, edible oils, fats & spreads & nutritional products. The Company has operations in Africa, Europe and Asia..

DIRS: R J Harvey (ch)*, G A Kanellis (ce), B H Leigh (fd), Ngozi Edozien*, Helen Owers*, Prof J A Arnold*, S J N Heale*, J T J Steel*, C G Davis (comml dir). **HEAD & REG OFF:** Manchester Business Park, 3500 Aviator Way, Manchester, M22 5TG. Tel: +44 1614351000 **REGISTRAR:** Computershare Investor Services PLC

BROKERS: J.P. Morgan Cazenove Ltd; Panmure Gordon (UK) Ltd. **FINANCIAL ADVISERS:** Citi. **AUDITORS:** PricewaterhouseCoopers LLP.

INTERIM: (29-Jan-13) 1/2 Year to 30 Nov 12. T/O £415m (£414m) Pre tax profit £40.6m (£39.3m) EPS 6.42p (6.33p) Int div 2.35p. (2.23p).. **OUTLOOK:** (14-Jun-12) Ann: '...the group remains confident that it will return to profitable growth in the new financial year'. (24-Jul-12) AR: ch - '...we are confident that the group will return to profitable growth in the current financial year'. (19-Sep-12) Ann: 'The board remains confident of a return to profitable growth in the current financial year'. (6-Dec-12) Ann: 'The board remains confident of a return to profitable growth in the current financial year'. (29-Jan-13) Int: 'The board remains confident of a return to profitable growth for the full year'. (11-Apr-13) Int: 'Results are expected to be in line with management expectations'.

NEWSFLOW: (5-Jan-12) Ann: The company announces the exchange of contracts for the acquisition through its beauty division of the Fudge hair care brand from Australian-based Sabre Group. The brand and associated inventory are being acquired for a consideration of £25.5m in cash with completion expected by the end of January following the satisfaction of certain regulatory obligations. (27-Mar-12) Ann: The company will announce a trading update on 14 June 2012, after the close of the financial year. (19-Sep-12) Ann: The company will announce a trading update on 06 December 2012. (20-Feb-13) Ann: The Company announces the exchange of contracts for the sale of its local Polish Home Care brands to Henkel. The Polish Home Care brands are being sold for a consideration of £46.6m in cash. Completion is subject to merger control clearances in Poland and Ukraine, processes that are anticipated to take approximately six months.

EPIC: PZC

ACTIVITIES ANALYSIS (12AR)

		T/O	Pr
Africa	%	42	55
Europe	%	39	89
Asia	%	19	-44

SHARE CAPITAL, HOLDINGS, DEALINGS

429m 1p Ord (Maj 49.7%, Dirs 0.21% [d]).

J B Zochonis	%	14.1
Zochonis Charitable Trust	%	11.6
M&G Group Ltd	%	11.6
Mrs C M Green Settlement	%	4.74
R J Harvey (ch)*	k	47.4 2+
G A Kanellis (ce)	k	439
B H Leigh (fd)	k	86.0
Helen Owers*	k	1.00
Prof J A Arnold*	k	13.5
S J N Heale*	k	8.00

PRICE (HMS 3) 26-APR-13			396p
market cap			£1,698m
position			164th
index			FTSE Mid 250
norm eps (pr)			18.5p
turnover (12AR)			£859m
pretax (12AR)			£48.5m

			m	s
DY (pr)	%	2.01	⊖	⊖
PER (pr)	x	21.5	⊖	⊖
PEG	f	na	⊕	⊕
GR (pr)	%	9.45	⊖	⊖
ROCE	%	26.2	⊖	⊖
MARGIN	%	12.3	⊖	⊖
GEAR	%	5.43	⊖	⊖
PBV	x	3.70	⊖	⊖
PTBV	x	6.09	⊖	⊖
PCF	x	48.7	⊖	⊖
PSR	x	1.97	⊖	⊖
PRR	x	484	⊖	⊖

nav ps (12AR) 107p
net cash ps (12AR) na

year ended 31 May		2008	2009	2010	2011	2012	2013E	2014E
turnover	£m	661	782	772	821	859		
depreciation	£m	15.7	17.5	18.8	21.6	22.5		
int paid (net)	£m	0.70	1.80	-0.40	-0.80	1.10		
FRS3 pretax	£m	76.5	84.4	102	106	48.5		
norm pretax	£m	68.8	89.8	103	109	104	107	117
turnover ps	£	1.55	1.83	1.81	1.92	2.01		
op margin	%	10.5	12.2	13.1	13.1	12.3		
ROCE	%	19.4	23.8	23.3	27.4	26.2		
ROE	%	10.0	12.3	12.9	13.0	14.9		
FRS3 eps	p	11.0	11.6	14.7	16.3	7.99		
norm eps	p	9.12	12.5	15.0	16.0	17.6	16.8	18.6
norm eps growth	%	-0.98	+37.5	+19.6	+6.93	+9.73	-4.64	+11.0
tax rate	%	27.6	27.1	29.0	26.2	21.6		
norm per	x					22.5	23.6	21.3
provisional peg	f							
cash flow ps	p	8.48	29.7	32.6	21.3	8.13		
capex ps	p	7.19	9.67	10.3	5.20	3.88		
dividend ps	p	4.34	4.81	6.02	6.09	6.72	7.29	8.04
dps growth	%	+10.0	+10.7	+25.1	+1.30	+10.2	+8.58	+10.2
dividend yield	%					1.70	1.84	2.03
dividend cover	x	2.11	2.62	2.53	2.67	2.63	2.30	2.32
shrholders funds	£m	349	390	455	474	458		
net borrowings	£m	32.3	-22.9	-86.2	-41.2	24.9		
net curr assets	£m	182	172	185	132	70.9		
ntav ps	p	45.8	54.2	68.1	56.0	49.0		

Broker	Date	Rec	2013 ESTIMATES			2014 ESTIMATES		
			Pretax £m	Eps p	Dps p	Pretax £m	Eps p	Dps p
Shore Capital	03-Aug-12	SELL	91.8 -	13.9 -	7.00 -	111 -	17.1 -	7.40 -
Milkstone Ltd	03-Aug-12	HOLD	98.0 -	15.5 -	7.25 -	115 +	18.2 +	8.00 +
Investec Securities	07-Mar-13	HOLD	105	16.2	7.39	116 -	18.0 -	8.13
Canaccord Genuity Ltd	11-Apr-13	SELL	108	17.4	7.40	123 +	19.9 +	8.10
Numis Securities Ltd	11-Apr-13	HOLD	108	17.1	7.05	122	19.5	8.20
Panmure Gordon	12-Apr-13	HOLD	105 +	16.8 +	7.22	115	18.5	7.76
		Consensus	**107**	**16.8**	**7.29**	**117**	**18.6**	**8.04**
	1m change		+0.82	+0.12	-0.01	+1.61	+0.01	+0.00
	3m change		+3.94	+0.89	+0.14	+13.9	+2.69	+0.89

GEARING, COVER (12AR)

		incl	Excl
intangibles		incl	Excl
net gearing	%	5.43	11.9
cash	%	14.4	31.4
gross gearing	%	19.8	43.3
under 5 yrs	%	19.8	43.3
under 1 yr	%	19.8	43.3
quick ratio	r		0.68
current ratio	r		1.22
interest cover	x		30.0

KEY DATES

next AR year end	31-May-13
int xd (2.23p)	22-Feb-12
year end	31-May-12
annual report	24-Jul-12
prelim results	24-Jul-12
fin xd (4.487p)	15-Aug-12
agm	19-Sep-12
int results	29-Jan-13
int xd (2.35p)	20-Feb-13
next agm	19-Sep-13

Source: JD Financial Publishing Ltd

options, but that is not good enough for me – I want to see real money invested, demonstrating belief and commitment (see 'Take your direction from the directors' below).

Take your direction from the directors

John Lee looks at the 'messages' sent to investors by board members' own shareholdings

For me, one of the most important investment indicators in decision-making relates to directors' shareholdings.

I like to see a plc board having a significant stake in its business, and I'm talking about an investment of their own resources – not just share options, although obviously these do provide an incentive.

Company annual reports must show individual director's shareholdings at both the current and previous year-ends, so it is easy to identify annual changes.

But the serious investor needs information much more promptly than that, ideally as soon as possible after transactions have taken place.

By law, any dealings done by a director have to be reported to the company and the stock exchange shortly after the transaction has been made.

Thus, the knowledge that a director has bought or sold quickly becomes public.

My bible, The Hemmington Scott Company REFS publication, to which I subscribe quarterly, has a section on director's dealings which I always study carefully.

What I look for in particular are deals done by a number of board members at roughly the same time – "cluster" transactions – because these send important messages to the investing community.

Clearly, a director has the inside track on knowledge about the company and an advantage over the outside investor.

Directors are legally barred from buying or selling before interim or final results, or if they are privy to important information such as a takeover approach, a favourable acquisition or the likelihood of a significant contract being won. Otherwise, they are free to make investment decisions just as we are.

To avoid any accusation of cherry-picking, I have looked back at all directors' cluster purchases involving main market plcs wth the initial 'A' for the past few months. Of the 20 such companies, in no less than 15 cases the directors concerned made a clear profit on their purchases. And of the other four – Allied Zurich, Arcadia, Arjo Wiggins and Astra Zeneca – those buying at the lower end of the price range also showed a profit.

While I accept that market conditions have been reasonably favourable, the overall outcome is striking in the extreme. The moral has to be: don't just watch directors' lips – watch where they put their savings.

Follow the leaders
Cluster share purchases by directors

Company	No. of directors buying	Date	Shares bought	Purchase price range (pence)	Price at Sep 10 (p)
AEA Technology	6	March/April	35,720	340/380	492.5
Airflow Streamlines	5	Feb/July	27,300	130/138	171
Airsprung Furniture	3	March/July	15,000	100/124	120.5
Allen	5	June/July	20,529	279/300	335
Allied Leisure	4	June/July	275,700	21.5/26.5	29.5
Allied Zurich	1	Feb/June	21,622	784/953	745
Alpha Airports	3	July	70,000	56.5/57	64
Amstrad	2	April/June	287,000	47/64	93.5
Anglian Water	5	May	5000	710	731.5
Anglo Pacific	3	April	606,200	14	23
Antofagasta Holdings	2	March/May	20,000	184/270	370
Arcadia Group	2	Feb/July	12,668	186/252	229.5
Arjo Wiggins Appleton	3	March/July	73,655	123/248	229.75
Ash and Lacy	2	May	9,900	119/120	152.5
Ashtenne Holdings	3	April/May	142,314	143/157	174.5
Associated British Ports	2	Feb/March	10,000	262/286	310.5
Astra Zeneca	5	April/May	108,450	2,419/2,531	2,422
Avesco	5	June	16,255	293/305	450
Avon Rubber	3	May	10,333	515	580
Azlan Group	2	Feb/May	70,000	53/77.5	79.5

Source: Author

Source: Lee, J. (1999) Take your direction from the directors, *Financial Times*, 11 December.

Author note

I would not invest in a PLC unless the directors themselves held serious personal shareholdings in it, and you shouldn't either. For me, the larger the better. Directors have to make their share transactions public and I watch these carefully, particularly when a number of directors of the same company are buying or selling, i.e. a cluster. This information is obtainable via the internet and publications such as *FT Money* and *Investors Chronicle*, which tabulate weekly directors' dealings, usually with comment. Sometimes there is a good reason for a director to sell, e.g. buying a house, meeting a capital gains tax bill, etc., but usually I am somewhat sceptical.

Let me say a word about non-executive directors. Ideally, we want to see quality, independent-minded non-executives who will robustly challenge the executives, but from my experience they are of varied quality. Too many, particularly in the smaller PLCs, are still chums of the executives or are retired former professional advisers.

Hardly a fool or a knave in sight

Well-publicised concern about the usefulness of non-executive directors does not worry John Lee

The long debate about the usefulness of non-executive directors tends to focus on big companies such as the Enrons and Marconis of this world. While majority opinion seems to favour an enhancement of the role and powers of non-execs, a vocal minority scorns them.

As an investor in the more established small cap stocks, somewhat different considerations apply to me. While I support the concept of non-execs, I do not exaggerate their importance, nor does their presence or absence particularly affect my investment decisions.

Many of my portfolio investments are in what I term "proprietorial" companies, which are in effect controlled by one family or individual. Here, small shareholders are in a very weak position and have to take a lot on trust.

However, far from feeling vulnerable, I usually feel much more secure, knowing that the key decision makers have their fortunes alongside my more modest pennies.

I also know that family members not in the business or who have considerable capital tied up in it and rely on dividend income to maintain their lifestyles.

The same more conservative attitude applies also to the level of directors' salaries and options. In my experience there is little abuse of power by such directors – few "fat cats" here. Indeed, at two annual meetings I have urged *increases* in remuneration and the establishment of a modest option scheme.

In contrast, many directors of large companies seem to spend more time on their salaries, options and bonuses than on running the business. Excessive corporate activity and clever off-balance-sheet financing techniques pose little threat to these directors if it all goes pear-shaped because their committed shareholding is often minimal.

Having said all this, non-execs do have a role and value in small companies, and gradually their standard and independence have improved. There are still family solicitors and local bank managers who contribute little, but these are gradually being replaced by achievers with track records in other companies.

I do not look to these non-execs to act as some form of superior internal auditor, but I do hope they will debate and discuss the merits of capital expenditure or acquisition proposals. I also like to think they will consider outside shareholders in dividend policy, the requirements of modern corporate governance and of course succession planning.

In addition, I would expect them to feed in their network of contacts and professional advisers to what could still be a somewhat insular "family" environment. With this type of company I do not find it unreasonable for non-execs to be agreeable and compatible. But I would expect them in an extreme situation to stand their ground, perhaps even to the point of resignation.

Ultimately it is the executive directors who run the business and, we hope, provide the drive, commitment and leadership; my investment is essentially in their hands. Today there are few fools running established profitable small companies and thankfully even fewer knaves.

Source: Lee, J. (2002) Hardly a fool or a knave in sight, *Financial Times*, 1 June.
© The Financial Times Limited 2002. All Rights Reserved.

Author note

I have been on the Board of a number of public companies over the years and generally have had a happy and, I hope, constructive tenure. However, on one occasion I resigned because I was unhappy with the chairman's attitude and his reluctance to separate the roles of chairman and chief executive. With another I was voted off by family shareholders' proxies, when I and the other non-executives questioned certain Board behaviour. One of my favourite jokes is: 'What is the difference between a supermarket trolley and a non-executive director?' Answer: 'While the supermarket trolley has got a mind of its own, you can get more food into a non-executive director.'

Nevertheless, at the end of the day it is the executive directors who are running the business and I try to meet them, form a judgement about their abilities, and as a long-term investor develop a relationship of trust with them.

Read their lips and accounts

Take a look at executives' body language, says John Lee

Leaving aside the rare knave or fool, most company chiefs take a responsible attitude to statements and comments they make on their companies' prospects. If profits are likely to be at variance with market forecasts, then public annoncements will have to be made.

However, rather more sensitive monitoring is needed for serious investors who try to keep in close touch with the companies whose shares they hold. For example, the attitude, phrases and words of chairmen and chief executives can be important indicators for the trained observer. I like to develop a "relationship" with my investments; this is something I have achieved over the years by attending AGMs and through phone discussions after results and other announcements.

Obviously in doing this, I have not taken advantage of any inside information or something told in confidence – either for personal dealing or in writing articles.

The idea is to build a relationship of mutual trust. Then, outside the obvious restrictions, one tries to assess information and make judgments. If, for example, a normally accessible company chief fails to return calls for days and is "locked in meetings", clearly something is up – perhaps takeover talks or a profits warning. As an investor, you need to try to make a judgment.

From my experience, good news and bad news are told in different ways. When things are going well the response to a question is immediate and often accompanied by a chuckle. When the news is bad, the reply is slower and the words more carefully constructed. The speaker wants to be truthful without causing depression or panic among investors.

One of my favourite questions when visiting a company is: "Where are you on an optimism scale of 1 – 10?" The response is often "11" accompanied by laughter, so sometimes a little discounting is necessary! I have repeatedly stressed the importance of attending annual meetings – not so much for the formal aspects but for the networking over coffee beforehand or the buffet afterwards.

You can have discussions with individual directors and the company's advisers, all of which will help you develop a "feel" for the current scene. At the AGM of Nichols, the food and drink company, I was told by two key people before the meeting: "Of course we are still a weather-dependent company".

Then the chairman said in his end-of-meeting statement that current trading was "OK, but we could do with a good summer." It was not difficult to deduce that trading was somewhat below budget, but not enough to warrant a profits warning.

Conversely, at the AGM of Lookers, my favourite motor distributor, chairman Fred Maguire was jovial and buoyant over pre-meeting coffee and pastries. I noticed, too, that he was wearing a much brighter tie than normal – perhaps a good omen.

Sure enough, we were told that "profits were well ahead of last year and in excess of budget" – clearly heading for a very good year.

Investing by watching screens is all very well, but you can't beat human contact. So get out there. Listen and observe, squeeze the flesh, study the eyes and the body language. It pays dividends if you make the effort.

 Source: Lee, J. (2001) Read their lips and accounts, *Financial Times*, 16 June.

Author note

Tell-tell signs from executives' behaviour.

Company visits and AGMs

I always like to visit prospective investments, to meet the executives in situ, to see the layout of the business, walk the shop floor or equivalent, and get a 'feel' for employees' attitudes and enthusiasm. Essentially what I am endeavouring to do is to build up a picture – a jigsaw – of a prospective PLC purchase, putting the things I see on a company visit, alongside the answers to my questions and alongside the financial data and statistics I have already gleaned. Hopefully it all fits together, but occasionally warning lights flash – the latest bright red Ferrari parked in prominent position outside the head office hardly inspires confidence. The following three articles record visits to three very different types of companies and my conclusions.

> ❝ build up a picture – a jigsaw – of a prospective PLC purchase ❞

A good prospect on paper

John Lee

The February snows had just cleared, leaving only a sprinkling on the hill-tops as I headed up the M6 to visit papermaker James Cropper near Kendal in the Lake District.

I had made a modest purchase in the company's shares earlier that month at 164p, attracted by its fundamentals. It was clearly a "proper" business with a 5 per cent yield and net assets of 320p – just like an old-time "assets situation". Its board is also optimistic – clearly further examination was called for.

Visiting a plc such as Cropper's is for me part of the interest and enjoyment of serious investing – an opportunity to embrace our industrial heritage and to appreciate the role that founding families and their businesses have played in the life of their communities. Tucked away by the bank of the River Kent lies the 20-acre Burneside mill complex that is James Cropper (established in 1845).

This is one of the oldest names in papermaking. The present fifth-generation chairman, James Cropper, lives close by – the annual report (it is worth becoming a shareholder just for the quality of paper) states:

"The company pays £26,250 annually to JA Cropper for the use of reservoirs to supply water to the factory premises ...".

It is a story of great commitment to a Lakeland community and of continuous innovation and capital investment – between 1976 and 1991, £43m was spent on re-equipment – today the company employs 500 people with a £30m turnover and significant exports.

There are four main divisions: speciality papers – the company is the largest manufacturer of bookbinding paper in the UK; converting – producing paper for picture frame mountings and display boards; technical fibre products – speciality non-woven materials from man-made mineral fibre, eg carbon, ceramic and glass, with a joint venture in the US plus a partnership programme with Johnson Matthey in fuel cell technology; finally a fast-growing chain of speciality paper shops – the nineteenth has just opened and 30 are planned, retailing 50 per cent Cropper products. All divisions are profitable.

When I visited, Cropper's stock market capitalisation was a paltry £14m. It is laughable to compare all this expertise and worth with some of the "hope and prayer" resource or drug discovery stocks with comparable capitalisations, floated primarily for promoter benefit.

Yet I accept that it is all about profits earned and dividends paid. Cropper's profits have fluctuated with a loss incurred in 2001, but the trend is now upwards. Dividends have also been solidly progressive with the annual report talking of rewarding shareholders "through progressive increases in dividends". Hopefully it is this that should steadily move the share price forward in time – the asset worth in this family-controlled company is somewhat academic, and its location is hardly a property hotspot. There is also a significant pension fund deficit to be tackled.

Nevertheless to quote finance director John Denman, Cropper is a "robust" business, gearing is modest, major capital expenditure has been completed, and its newer technologies offer longer term spice.

I was sufficiently enthused to add to my holding after the visit – not easy given the tight market. A subsequent upbeat trading statement moved the shares forward to around 190p with the yield down to 4 per cent.

Profits growth for the year to March 2006 should deliver a price/earnings ratio of just into double figures. Not in the bargain basement short term, but hopefully a genuine "lock-away". I personally feel much more comfortable prospecting on the banks of The Kent than The White Nile!

Source: Lee, J. (2005) A good prospect on paper, *Financial Times*, 2 April.

Author note

In the end I did not hold Cropper's for more than a few months, making just a small profit, as I decided that there were more exciting opportunities elsewhere. I sold out between 175p and 225p – today, eight years later, they are around 310p, hardly the most exciting of performances. As the saying goes: 'One day Cropper's time will come but many shareholders will have died waiting.'

Raise a glass to a solid earner

John Lee

To Stockton-on-Tees to spend the day with Brulines "the leading provider of real-time minitoring systems and data management services for the leisure and forecourt services sectors". This interesting, but relatively unknown, company floated on the Alternative Investment Market (Aim) in 2006 at 123p – and I have since made 11 separate purchases between 80p and 96p to build up my holding.

James Dickson, the chief executive, has been in the market, too. Last month, he bought 50,000 shares at 84p to take his total holding up to just under 4m shares – or 14 per cent of the company's £26m market capitalisation.

Brulines' core monitoring and information systems are installed in nearly 20,000 UK pubs – nearly one in every three – covering their drink and gaming equipment. Its fuel equipment is even more popular – being used by 60 per cent of retailers by volume, which should help the division move into profit next year. Overall, recurring revenues across the group now account for 70 per cent of turnover.

I was also impressed with the technology and the enthusiasm of the team helping to generate new opportunities. Whitbread's Costa and Coffee Nation chains are clients and Brulines is in negotiation with Visa Europe to provide contactless payment technology in vending machines.

With pre-tax profits forecast to be £4m for the year to 31 March 2012, Brulines' shares trade on a modest price/earnings ratio of 9 times, and offer a chunky dividend yield of 6.25 per cent.

I believe this is a solid group poised for growth. It is likely to become better known and, I hope, re-rated over the next few years – while paying a nice dividend in the meantime.

However, apart from Brulines, I have done little buying recently. With markets moving upwards, I have not spotted many really attractive opportunities, thus I have confined myself to one or two "add-ons".

I have held Air Partner, the world's leading air charter broker, for many years. But its shares have frequently suffered mid-air turbulence! I first bought the shares around the £2 mark in 1999, then sold some at £3 in 2001-2 and some more, from within my personal equity plan, at £11.40 in 2007. They peaked at £14 later that year.

In spite of volatile trading conditions, the company has always been cash positive and, even when issuing a cautious trading statement, indicated cash balances of £13m out of a £28m market capitalisation. I have added more at 280p and 285p for my individual savings acount (Isa).

Another "old friend" presenting an attractive opportunity was the Leeds-based property company Town Centre. Its interim results last month revealed an overall portfolio letting rate of 97 per cent, so I was delighted to buy the shares at 139p, again for my Isa, at around half net asset value and with a 7 per cent yield. They have recovered to 170p

Looking across my other holdings, four hover around all-time "highs" – Delcam, Fenner, Nichols and S&U. But there have been disappointing trading statements from Norcros – thankfully only a small holding – and, more importantly, from Gooch & Housego, following a fall in orders for their industrial lasers. However, there were good results and much-appreciated dividend increases from Primary Health Properties, publisher Quarto, and agricultural feedstuffs/country/pet stores group Wynnstay. My largest holding, Treatt – the flavours and fragrances company – also reported improving orders in January and February.

Source: Lee, J. (2012) Raise a glass to a solid earner, *Financial Times*, 3 March.

Author note

Brulines, now renamed Vianet, has been a tad disappointing so far but I am keeping faith; apparently some important contract negotiations have taken longer than anticipated. However, it has maintained its dividend and prime mover James Dickson has further increased his already substantial shareholding.

Anpario provides some food for thought

John Lee

A bright, warm August morning saw me snaking through the Peak District to visit Aim-traded Anpario at its Manton Wood Enterprise Park headquarters at Worksop, Nottinghamshire.

I had been aboard since buying in January at 82p, previously met chief executive David Bullen (ex-Novartis) and finance director Karen Prior, and had promised myself a visit during the Parliamentary recess.

Although a younger plc than I usually back – it was only founded in 1996 and admitted to Aim in 2005 – Anpario possesses the ingredients I look for; strong committed management, debt-free, cash-positive, growing profitably with progressive dividend, and an international spread turnover. The business "formulates, produces and sells high-performance natural animal feed additives to over 70 countries". The sales mix is approximately 50 per cent European, 25 per cent Asia Pacific, 10 per cent Middle East Asia, 10 per cent Latin America and 5 per cent Africa. Last year saw particularly strong trading performances in Argentina, Bangladesh, Japan, Korea, Malaysia, Mexico and Turkey; future trading initiatives will focus on China and Brazil, which between them account for more than 40 per cent of world pig and poultry meat production.

A recent acquisition, Meriden, has a strong presence in China, supplying 16 of the top 20 feed mills there. Fundamental drivers should benefit Anpario; a growing world population, plus legislation working in favour of natural additives and away from antibiotic growth promoters. Additionally, the global feed market is very fragmented and although there are large players such as BASF, Bayer and Nutreco, there are also many smaller companies successful in niche additives which provide acquisition opportunties.

On my visit I was pleased to be joined by my younger daughter, Elspeth, who has a career in nutrition, for technical advice and questioning. Following a briefing with Prior, executive vice-chairman Richard Edwards (ex-Saint-Gobain), and senior technical staff we toured the relatively small freehold site, which is currently only 50 per cent utilised; Anpario operates another plant in North Yorkshire.

At about £1 a share, the company is only capitalised at £19m on a price/earnings ratio of 9.5 and its shares yield 2.5 per cent on a well-covered dividend. Provided its acquisition policy is cautious and conservative I see little downside. Five years hence it should be significantly larger, likely to be increasingly attractive to a hungry global player. I have added to my shareholding, despite it being a very tight market, and Elspeth bought for her portfolio too. Anpario's 2012 interim results are expected on September 19.

Turning to other holdings, performance has been encouraging. No real nasties, but some pleasing performances from Delcam, James Fisher, S&U and VP with an upward re-rating taking place steadily in Smiths News.

Finally, there have been fun and games with defence flares and decoys maker Chemring. I thought I had bought well recently at £3, but a fortnight later private equity firm Carlyle made a preliminary approach and the shares surged £1. However, a profits warning this week saw a sharp reversal – so I made a speedy, modestly profitable exit at £3.28p.

 Source: Lee, J. (2012) Anpario provides some food for thought, *Financial Times*, 1 September.
© The Financial Times Limited 2012. All Rights Reserved.

Author note

I bought AIM-quoted Anpario on 12 occasions during 2012, at between 80p and 105p. On the back of very positive results and a dividend increase, its shares have travelled well. I foresee considerable growth ahead for Anpario and then expect it to be gobbled up by a larger player.

I obviously accept that for me, wearing the additional hat of a financial journalist, arranging a company visit is relatively easy, although I suspect that private investors may well be pleasantly surprised by their reception if they did attempt to visit more of their shareholdings. But there are no such limitations or restrictions on AGM attendance – AGMs are open to all shareholders. I have attended dozens over the years – one can learn a lot not necessarily from what is said in the formal part of the meeting but from private discussions with the Board, etc. pre or post, and attendance also gives a feel for a company's culture and personalities.

Time at an AGM is time well spent

John Lee finds that private investors can gain a great deal if they adopt the right approach

The accepted view of company annual general meetings is that they are a necessary chore: five minutes of formal resolutions; rarely a question from shareholders; 20 minutes of light conversation and then back to serious business.

I take a rather different view and, as a private investor, relish AGMs as a real opportunity to form a view of the board members and to gain knowledge. Through attending these meeting, I have gained financially, had many amusing interludes, tucked into some excellent buffets and picked up at least one non-executive directorship.

The psychology of AGMs is important to understand. The chairman is usually apprehensive, having spent hours with advisers preparing for difficult questions that might arise. Will the recently fired sales manager turn up to wreak his revenge?

Usually, of course, nothing untoward happens and the meeting progresses without incident. The chairman relaxes, defences down. This is the ideal time for a shareholder to move into action.

Take careful note of expressions, reactions, nuances – all valuable information. If the chairman is the dominant shareholder, any lack of family succession points to a future takeover.

I recall, years ago, turning up to the annual meeting in London of Goldrei Foucard, a baking ingredient manufacturer. I came away with the knowledge that there was no next generation to the very nice chairman. So, I bought more shares – and was rewarded by a takeover within weeks.

Sometimes, you see clashes within families. At a Birmingham AGM, the chairman, while giving a carefully crafted and cautious statement on trading conditions, was interrupted by his brother who, sitting alongside, proclaimed loudly that things actually were rather better than that. They scowled at each other for the rest of the meeting.

Major institutions rarely attend AGMs (having their own private briefings) so the meetings are the private investors' theatre. But be strong-willed. Do not waste the time in which you could be gathering crucial information by going back for a second helping at the buffet. Circulate – and make sure you stay sober.

Gaining entry to AGMs usually presents no difficulty – many companies are delighted just to have a shareholder turn up. Some have a table at the door on which sits an enormously inhibiting copy of the share register. However a look of authority, or saying rather grandly that your holding is in "nominee" names, usually suffices.

Be sure that you arrive early. Some members of the board normally do and are only too happy to talk with you, particularly if they are coming up for re-election that day.

At the worst, you might have to make do with the company secretary. But they can be a good ally to have, probably fielding any follow-up telephone calls that you might make.

The success, growth and integrity of the company (and thus your investment) is tied inextricably to the personality, abilities and ambitions of the chairman and/or chief executive.

If he owns a flashy BMW with personalised number plates, drips with gold jewellery and has ambitions to own the local football club – bad news. But a conservative car, gentlemen's shoes, love of cricket, faded regimental tie and membership of the local school board spell good news.

I exclude from all this the 30-year-old, multi-millionaire, whiz-kid creators of IT companies on price/earnings ratios of 50-plus. These live on a different planet from me, anyway, so normal judgments and personality tests do not apply.

To sum up: attending an AGM is much more valuable than many investors imagine. It is time well spent.

Most are at a sensible time and venue. But if you are daft enough to stick with a company that holds its AGM on Boxing day in John O'Groats, then you have only yourself to blame.

 Source: Lee, J. (1999) Time at an AGM is time well spent, *Financial Times*, 15 May.
© The Financial Times Limited 1999. All Rights Reserved.

Author note

I think this article is self-explanatory – I would definitely encourage AGM attendance whenever possible.

At least I made the buffet

Sometimes the toughest challenge is to operate the tea and coffee flasks by John Lee

Over the years I have attended countless AGMs in company offices, hotel suites and boardrooms all over the country. Too often what should be the one real opportunity of the year to build bridges between the board and the private investor becomes a rather short and soulless formal event – a lost opportunity for both.

These days most chairmen rely on a carefully honed and scripted cribsheet with even the proposers and seconders of resolutions carefully chosen and primed; usually the chairman is in a state of high tension and anxiety, wondering whether difficult questions will be asked.

For the average shareholder who bothers to attend, the biggest challenge is to operate the large tea and coffee flasks on the back table without accidentally pouring hot liquid everywhere.

Gaining access to the meeting presents little problem; by the entrance usually sits an over-awed secondee from the typing pool behind an enormously imposing copy of the share register. Waving a copy of the report and accounts, or rather more importantly, announcing that your shares are in nominee names will usually get you in.

Most AGMs are over in minutes with rarely a question asked. The chairman grandly announces that the resolution to reappoint him has 10m proxy votes in favour with only 300 against.

There are smiles and titters as everyone speculates on the indentity of the minority votes. Probably a shareholder has just put the X in the wrong box.

Occasionally one encounters an anoraked shareholder intent on asking convoluted questions from a large notepad and frequently referring to "our company", causing everyone to search for some obscure point about Page 23, Subsection (c).

Initially tolerant, everyone eventually gets bored then irritated until the shareholder is finally silenced by the chairman around question 8 with the offer of further discussions after the meeting.

AGMs can have their own humour; some years ago in Birmingham, the chairman, while giving a carefully crafted and cautious statement on trading conditions, was interrupted by his brother who, sitting alongside, proclaimed loudly that things were actually rather better than that.

On another occasion I remember hurrying to the Metalrax AGM. Rounding the final corner a minute before the start I ran smack into a funeral cortege moving at snail's pace, led by a black coated attendant on foot. I missed the formal meeting, thankfully I made the buffet.

For me the AGM is an important date in the calendar – an opportunity to assess the board, to mix and talk in the margins of the meeting, adding to ones knowlege of the company and its personalities; to assess next year's prospects and to check on issues such as dividend policy and whether there is a family succession issue.

Last year I attended the London AGM of specialist insurance broker Windsor. I liked the feel of the company and what I heard, and afterwards confidently bought more holdings. Last week's AGM reported further progress and optimism. Between the two meetings its shares have appreciated significantly.

Companies could do much more to encourage shareholders to attend their AGMs. Apart from food and small gifts they could consider mounting product displays and presentations, perhaps with videos of activities and overseas operations. Meetings could be made much livelier and more exciting.

Private investors all too frequently miss out on this unique opportunity to gain knowledge.

Source: Lee, J. (2003) At least I made the buffet, *Financial Times*, 15 February.
© The Financial Times Limited 2003. All Rights Reserved.

Author note

Nothing more to add!

As well as possible company visits and AGM attendance, modest private sleuthing is both sensible and acceptable. I remember visiting a couple of HMV stores and talking, as a shopper, to staff. There were enough doubts and negatives to have discouraged me from investing, but I foolishly ignored them and paid the price. You must always be rational and not let the heart rule the head, i.e. sometimes you just *want* to believe that a share you have discovered is worth buying and you want your further investigations

❝you must always be rational and not let the heart rule the head❞

to be positive, to justify purchase. This happened with HMV – I didn't remain sufficiently detached and rational. I reveal more of my failures in Chapter 7, 'My mistakes'.

If a company attracts me, I make contact with its company secretary or registrars to ask for a copy of the latest annual report. These reports give a substantial amount of information on the PLC, apart from the accounts themselves. Although much of the detail may well be of limited interest to the amateur investor, the chairman's and/or chief executive's comments on future trading should be seriously studied.

Constructing a portfolio

Few investors apply much consistency or logic to the creation of their personal investment portfolios. Your average investor will usually hold a range of stocks, with substantially differing values, delivering wildly varying yields, with no obvious theme or structure. Often there is a mix of a few small-value privatisation or mutualisation holdings, a number bought on the basis of 'well worth a punt' tips from city columns, 'gossip' recommendations which have done the rounds at the 19th hole of the golf club, perhaps a share bought through sitting next to a director on the return holiday flight, maybe the favourite retailer frequently visited by your wife or partner, plus a number of personal hunches. In truth, a bit of a dog's breakfast!

This type of portfolio is unlikely to make your fortune – performance will probably be little better than average. Put very simply, to give an extreme example, if a portfolio has only, say, three holdings, one worth £50,000 and two each worth less than £1,000, the performance of the two small holdings will be virtually irrelevant compared with that of the £50,000 holding. It is crucial to ensure that holdings you have great confidence in are of sufficient value to make a real difference to your overall result.

> **ensure holdings you have great confidence in are of sufficient value to make a real difference**

Some investment commentators believe that there is a clear division between 'income', i.e. shares which deliver good and regular dividend payouts, and 'growth' stocks, i.e. here the dividend yield is low, perhaps minuscule, with the PLC focusing on retention of profits – ploughing them back for future growth which investors believe will be significant.

I have always believed that as an investor you should look for shares providing both, and that there is an obvious relationship between the two. In Chapter 4, when talking about valuations, I said that I looked for a reasonably attractive dividend yield, ideally 5%+, and a single-figure price earnings ratio. However, I have to concede that shares like this, often in long-established PLCs, are a disappearing breed, and in the future investors may have to accept lower initial dividend yields than they could have obtained in the past.

How big should your portfolio be?

Among investors there is disagreement about the number of shares you should have in a portfolio, with endless arguments using too many clichés between spreading the risk and having too many eggs in one basket. In my current portfolios, putting together my ISA and non-ISA holdings, I hold around 35 different stocks. There is no particular magic about '35', although curiously many private investors seem to find this a comfortable number of holdings to have: keeping track of significantly more holdings can be quite demanding.

My stocks vary significantly in value, probably by a factor of up to 10. This is for two reasons:

1   In some cases shares I own are in the early stages of build-up and I need to know more about them before adding further. This is something I'll do when I have gained greater confidence in those holdings.

2   As with a number of my larger holdings, they have grown substantially over the years. With many small cap stocks where there is often a limited market in their shares I have to make up to a dozen or more purchases before building to the size of holding I desire.

I do not bother with overseas holdings, nor am I concerned about asset or sector allocation – I am focused on particular stocks. Let me explain my reasons.

If you're a manager of large institutional funds you'll usually aim for X% in the USA, Y% in South East Asia, Z% in Europe, etc., and similarly a certain percentage in banks and financial stocks, another in media, and yet another in healthcare, etc., and this is the right approach. But I believe that the private investor should forget about all this for their more modestly sized portfolios. I like UK-headquartered and quoted businesses which operate internationally anyway as they seek world markets for their products or services. If I look at my four current largest holdings – Delcam, Nichols, PZ Cussons and Treatt – they all generate significant profits abroad. However, I do have one or two holdings, such as Smiths News in newspapers/periodicals distribution and Wynnstay in agricultural services, which are overwhelmingly UK centred.

> **❝ I like UK-headquartered and quoted businesses which operate internationally ❞**

Attitude to risk

Before embarking on an equity journey and building up your portfolio, it is important to decide how much capital you wish to allocate. All equity or ordinary share investment carries a degree of risk and you should work out how much you are prepared to risk. I believe that everyone should keep a reserve of liquidity outside their portfolio to meet family emergencies. While a portfolio can be part liquidated relatively quickly, there have been times, such as the secondary banking crisis of the early 1970s or the 2008 subprime/banking crash, when markets have plunged and stocks have become almost unsaleable. In addition, for someone predominantly invested in small cap shares, you have to be conscious of a tighter or more restricted market, thus patience may be required when attempting to realise cash.

I'd also advise that there is no need to invest all your equity allocation in one splurge. Take time over it, build up the portfolio at a pace that you feel happy with as and when you go 'nap' on (select) a particular share.

The degree of risk an investor is prepared to take clearly varies from individual to individual. Put very simply, the scale of risk can be anything from very high risk biotech or exploration stocks (great if they come off, but invariably near-total losses if they fail and therefore not for me) to relatively safe, established companies like Dignity in funerals, Diageo in spirits, Tesco in retailing and Unilever in household products. Of course, the latter can move up or down in price depending on their profitability and the general performance of the stock market, but losses here are likely to be much more limited and certainly an investor will not lose everything.

One of my cardinal principles has been to focus on avoiding losses rather than chasing profits. In golf it is the shot in the river or wood that destroys the round; similarly with investing – it is the portfolio losses that drag down an overall performance.

Investment fashion – the rational and the irrational

Share price movements, in my experience, tend to be more rational than irrational, but sometimes an excess of rational buying can propel prices upwards to an unsustainable and unrealistic level. If we look back at three very different sectors – pharmaceuticals, supermarkets and mobile telephony – you will see what I mean.

In the past all were regarded as great growth sectors, for obvious reasons, and rated accordingly. Yields on leading shares in these areas were low as share prices rose on the expectation of sustained growth – Vodafone at one stage was yielding only around 1%. Investors who bought in early did well, but those who arrived late would unquestionably have lost money as these sectors went 'ex-growth'. Pharmaceuticals saw governments becoming increasingly unwilling to pay high prices for drugs, generic competition increased and research and development (R&D) successes became fewer. Our towns became supermarket saturated and heavily competitive, with communities growing increasingly resilient to yet more supermarket developments which they saw as destroying the high street. Similarly, the mobile phone marketplace became progressively more difficult as competition from new providers offering cheaper tariffs increased and a greater percentage of the population owned a mobile phone.

Thus former growth stocks moved downwards on to much lower ratings, dividend yields correspondingly rose, and the investment community increasingly viewed them as income rather than growth stocks. I steered well clear when prices were high, but happily bought into Vodafone in 2009 at 122p when it was yielding around 6%, taking a tax-free 'turn' in my ISA at 163p in 2011. They have since moved further ahead, primarily on the realisation of their holding in Verizon of the USA. My conservative approach keeps me well clear of buying stocks on minuscule yields and PERs of 20+.

From time to time a niche investment sector will suddenly excite investors and they will pile in almost herd-like. In November 1997 I bought 5,000 shares in Nord Anglia – a North Western company operating children's nurseries and private education establishments – at 187.5p. It was then announced that the company had been awarded certain government training contracts. Whoosh! Favourable media comment and buying in a relatively tight market saw Nord Anglia shares rise dramatically – I departed four months later at an unbelievable 437p. They hardly ever saw this price again. Sadly, poor management and a disastrous acquisition brought a collapse in the share price and ultimately the company was bought out.

> **ff from time to time a niche investment sector will suddenly excite investors JJ**

It was the world of the internet which demonstrated the irrationality and gullibility of investors and the dangers of following the herd. For a time any company which developed a website or any flotation which suggested internet/web involvement was chased by investors to crazy levels. I kept well away, apart from a brief flirtation in February 2000 when my broker was handling the flotation of something rather touchingly called Just 2 Clicks. I agreed to take some for a punt at 150p. I got 6,666 shares, speedily turning them over a week later at 250p. Just 2 Clicks had no real business – it was all hope and prayer and definitely not my bag. I ended my January 2000 *FT* 'My Portfolio' article with these words: 'I will never be a "day-trader". When there is a blow-out in many of the absurdly over-priced internet stocks, the tears will not be mine.'

Many speculators made substantial monies on the way up, but much blood was spilled on the way down. The lesson to be learned is: tread very warily when following 'fashion' and avoid getting swept up by euphoria.

When to exit or when to stay

Whether you are a professional or a private investor, when to sell is one of the most difficult decisions to take, and in truth it is an area which is very difficult to give guidance on. It is relatively easy if you are losing on a particular stock. My advice is to apply a 20% stop-loss, i.e. sell shares if they fall 20% below the original purchase price. By all means allow a company one mistake, but then draw the line. Not only will selling and taking the loss on the chin be arguably the correct course financially, it will also, and if not more importantly, clear the decks and restore confidence. There is nothing more debilitating than studying your portfolio and being reminded daily of investing mistakes. You need to accept the loss as soon as possible and move on. Every investor makes mistakes but usually investors only want to talk about their successes, so don't be fooled. I devote the next chapter to my mistakes and sadly there have been too many!

If you have profitable holdings, my general approach is to let profits run. Don't sell if you are invested in a company delivering profits and dividend growth year on year. Most of my mistakes have been in selling too soon, although uncomfortably there have been bad selections as well. In the investing world there is wildly different advice: some advisers say sell half a successful holding so the balance stands you in nil cost. Then there is an old Rothschild saying: 'I made my money by selling too soon', i.e. not being too greedy. But generally I would let profits run.

However, most growing companies will experience a pause in profits growth. Be patient, stay aboard, don't lose faith. Only if a holding becomes too 'toppy' – too over-priced – should you sell. Or, of course, if you believe that the company's future is either really uncertain or has worsened dramatically.

❝ most growing companies will experience a pause in profits growth ❞

Above all, put time into the equation. The biggest mistake private investors make is to constantly chop and change. It might make your broker happy but you won't make your million that way.

As the legendary Warren Buffett famously said: 'Lethargy bordering on sloth remains the cornerstone of our investment style.' Definitely an attitude to be encouraged.

My mistakes

Every investor needs to be upfront and honest about their mistakes. As I said in Chapter 2, as an investor you should take a loss and move on. In this chapter I'm going to tell you about my investing errors and show you what I learned, and what you can learn from them.

My mistakes fall into two clear categories: stocks sold far too soon and individual stocks just sadly misjudged. It is the former category which unquestionably has been the more costly. However, in mitigation I have to make the point that with limited capital for many years, my policy was to take profits, probably pay CGT and use the net proceeds both to provide the extras in my life, such as holidays, antiques and paintings, and to generate new resources for the next wave of investment ideas. While it may be ideal, in financial terms, to reinvest all profits, it is important to recognise that there is more to life than the stock market and creating personal wealth. My late father jokingly used to say that money was not for spending but for buying shares. Realistically, most private investors probably need or prefer to spend the dividends they receive to have a life – there is not much fun in being the richest person in the graveyard! If, however, you can afford to reinvest dividends, particularly in a tax-free ISA, then this should be encouraged.

> if you can afford to reinvest dividends ... this should be encouraged

Where I went wrong

Take new issues first. In 1967 I obtained 100 shares in William Morrison Supermarket at 27s.6d, selling out the next day at 34 shillings for a profit of £30. How wrong I was. What would this holding be worth today after 45 years of growth?

In 1983, in the privatisation, I was successfully allocated 100 Associated British Ports at 112p, selling out in 1986 for 555p. Yes, a fine profit, but ABP has proved the most profitable by far of all the privatisation issues – something like a 70-fold appreciation over the years before finally succumbing to a takeover. If only ...

Yet it is the memory of a number of larger value holdings, sold much too soon, that pains me the most. In 1972 I invested £19,000 in 60,000 Bodycote shares, then a small textiles/industrial holdings group. From memory it was just about to acquire its first heat-treatment company. I had invested far more than I normally do then. I couldn't afford to hold and turned them over on a dip in the market for a loss of £3,000. Over the next 40 years Bodycote has become a world leader in the heat-treatment sector and is capitalised today at over £1 billion. I would rather not know what my holding would be worth now!

Next a similar 'lost fortune' with advertising/media WPP. In December 1984 I alighted on a small East Anglian-quoted manufacturer of supermarket baskets and cages for animal experimentation, Wire and Plastic Products. I invested £9,000, convinced that one day something would happen. Early the following year a certain Martin Sorrell arrived on the scene – I confess to never having heard of him then! He bought a block of shares – it appeared that he was going to develop it as his vehicle. The shares shot up. I gleefully sold in mid-1985 for a total of £26,000, well content. Today WPP, as a multinational advertising and media group, is worth £16 billion. Well done, Martin, big fool John. But how was I to know?

Croda was another Lee miss. £2,000 invested at 73p a share in 1982, sold for a princely profit of £56. Today the shares stand around £25. Border TV was a share I bought in 1992, convinced that as a regional TV tiddler it would be gobbled up by a larger player. Sadly I lost patience with it, although I still profitably sold out my £5,000 holding six years later for £17,000 at 346p. Had I held on for just two more years I would have exited at no less than £14 after a takeover battle – see 'Investment lessons in a tough school' below.

Investment lessons in a tough school

John Lee feels he has learned plenty after being on the receiving end of many bids over the years

What do engineering group Charter and textiles company Courtaulds have in common? Both recently received takeover bids at 100 per cent premiums to their market share prices.

That was nice work if you had bought the shares only recently. But, for long-termers, it was only a limited recompense for years of distinctly lacklustre investment performance.

Nevertheless, for a value investor like myself, takeover bids provide at least an acknowledgement of the real worth of companies. Over the years, I have been on the receiving end of many bids and have learned several hard lessons:

■ Be patient and back your own judgment. Don't be tempted to take profits too soon before a likely bid.

■ It usually pays to see a bid situation through to the end. A rival bid often appears, and there is nearly always a premium paid for a recommended bid.

■ Do not be tempted to take loan stock or similar as consideration purely to defer or avoid capital gains tax liabilities. This ties up capital for a longish period.

I prefer to take the tax hit, so freeing resources to take advantage of new investment opportunities.

Looking back, my worst mistake was in March 1998 when I decided to take profits on half a dozen shareholdings, including Border Television.

I had bought Border in 1992 at 107p, on a yield of 6 per cent plus, believing that a larger media predator would appear one day, and I took a nice profit six years later at 346p. Now, after a keenly-fought battle, Border has just been taken out at £14 a share.

Sometimes, I kick myself for not buying in the first place. I always believed that tennis/leisure centre operator David Lloyd would attract a predator, and was not surprised when Whitbread pounced. On the other hand, I was convinced that Smith and Nephew would have lost its independence years ago.

In recent times, my portfolio has achieved two or three good bids each year. Bridport, an air cargo restraint specialist; Trafford Park Estates; and Henry Cooke, my main broker, have been significant successes. I was particularly fortunate to have Bray Technology, a Leeds-based maker of gas burners, taken over within six months of my purchase.

One of my core holdings at present is Breedon, a quarrying and housebuilding group that I bought at the end of 1998. It has just agreed a 180p cash bid from Ennstone – a 100 per cent profit.

I have the proceeds of the Royal London/United Assurance deal waiting for reinvestment within my personal equity plan. In addition, Landround, a niche travel incentive promoter quoted on the Alternative Investment Market, is in talks that, with luck, will end happily.

Spotting bid targets is never easy. Financial services, pharmaceuticals and telecommunications continue to be obvious areas for consolidation.

I also expect activity in department stores, leisure clubs, motor distributors, and smaller hotel and property companies with share prices representing sizeable discounts to net assets.

Bids tend to be rarer in what I term "proprietorial" plcs where there are significant family shareholdings, with the present generation "stewarding" the business for the next.

Corporate activity here is more likely to take the form of a "buy-in" where the dominant shareholders take the company private, with a much lower premium being offered than with a third-party bid.

Be alert, however, to family companies where there are no obvious successors and where a deal seems likely at some stage.

For the ideal bid opportunity, look for small, well managed businesses in sectors dominated by much larger and wealthier groups. Like Border Television, these should offer profitable journeys, hopefully with a crock of gold at the end.

Source: Lee, J. (2000) Investment lessons in a tough school, *Financial Times*, 13 May.
© The Financial Times Limited 2000. All Rights Reserved.

Author note

In this article, written in 2000, I say that 'in recent times, my portfolio has achieved two or three good bids each year'. However, in recent years merger and acquisition (M&A) activity has slowed down markedly – now it is more like one bid per year, with buyers being considerably more cautious and focusing on conserving their resources.

My final 'scar' in this selling-too-soon saga concerns the world-leading shipbroker Clarkson (see article below).

Profit-taking with a catch

John Lee

My annual salmon fishing week on the Tweed near Kelso always gives me the opportunity to relax and reflect on my investment strategy. This year, though, there were few fresh fish, few new jokes to share with Kenny the head gillie and few new investment ideas.

The lack of new ideas is hardly surprising given the very considerable rises in my type of small-cap value stocks. It really has been a fabulous period.

For me, equity investment is about long-term growth in both capital and income. I have never worried too much about annual performance comparisons, though obviously recent returns have been very satisfying.

I am now very reluctant to pay capital gains tax through taking profits in my main portfolio. But within my tax-free Peps and Isas I will "topslice" at times where a holding has raced ahead to unsustainable levels in the short term or has become disproportionately large.

This decision, when a stock keeps rising, is amongst the most difficult to take. A classic example of this has been Clarkson, the world's leading shipping broker. Shipping has long been a notoriously cyclical industry and the company's earnings fluctuated, but it always had a strong cashflow and paid a dividend.

I bought into it in November 2002 at 149p on an incredible 10 per cent yield – a wonderful Peps/Isas scoop. I bought more at 170p and more again early last year at up to 228p. Investors were waking up to the tremendous rise in freight rate powered by China's economic growth; arguably Clarksons was becoming the best and safest play on China's boom.

➡

On and on the shares climbed through the £4 barrier and then towards £5. I asked myself frequently how long this could go on, torn as I was between banking part of my profit and my fundamental investment belief that one usually does better to stay aboard for the long term.

I finally decided to topslice a fifth of my holding at 488p this January, telling myself that nothing goes up for ever. Hardly pausing for breath, off went Clarkson again, leaving me agonising about what to do as I drove up to Scotland with the shares at 550p and the yield down to 3 per cent.

Freight rates were (and are) still very high, and the company's coming annual results would clearly be excellent. Furthermore, the way they earn their commissions over the duration of a contract substantially underpins earnings for at least the next couple of years. Against this, many investors were sitting on large profits and the slightest negative hint on freight rates or China could precipitate a sharp reaction.

In the end my innate caution prevailed, and an early call to my broker before heading from hotel to river saw another fifth of my holding sold at 550p. The tragic news of the Madrid bombings knocked prices towards the end of the week, since when they have hovered just above £5. Bonanza results this week – a near tripling of profits – should underpin the shares. But a repeat tripling of the share price is hardly realistic.

The week's fishing brought me just one fine 7lb fish, although the environmental programme necessitated me returning it to the river, for which I received a Tweed Foundation sweatshirt – probably the most expensive such garment ever. My investment activities during the week have, of course, created useful liquidity in my Peps and Isas for reinvestment, but like those elusive salmon, undervalued stocks are currently very hard to find.

 Source: Lee, J. (2004) Profit-taking with a catch, *Financial Times*, 3 April. © The Financial Times Limited 2004. All Rights Reserved.

Author note

A classic example of selling a fine company far too soon! Having first bought Clarkson at 149p, it would have turned into a 'ten bagger' if only I had stayed aboard. Here in 2004 I write, with the shares around £5, 'a repeat tripling of the share price is hardly realistic'. Well, that was precisely what happened and I couldn't have been more wrong. They are now approaching £20!

I spotted it in 2002, buying at 149p on what now seems an incredible 10% yield. I visited this old, established shipping services company at its city headquarters, spending some time with the then finance director, to learn more about it. Subsequently I formed a friendship with the chairman, Tim Harris, pleasantly dining with him on many occasions over the years. He was also chairman of marine services James Fisher, of which more in the next chapter. By 2003 I grew increasingly confident about Clarkson, a great cash-generating business, and I made eight separate purchases, building my holding to a total of 50,000 shares.

Tim used to warn me of shipping's famous cycle. Thus I could not resist the banking of a good profit. I sold steadily between 2004 at 485p and 2009 at 1030p. In an *FT* article of 2004, with Clarkson shares standing around £5, I wrote: '... a near tripling of profits should underpin the shares. But a repeat tripling of the share price is hardly realistic.' Nearly 10 years later Clarkson are approaching £20!

❝ put time into the equation, one of my absolutely key investment cornerstones ❞

Hopefully readers can now understand why I plead with them to be patient, to put time into the equation, one of my absolutely key investment cornerstones. Although shipping cycles are well documented, I had not fully appreciated what a growth industry shipping is – recent projections indicate still further long-term growth.

Failures that could have been avoided

I now turn to the many individual shares where I have lost money. These failures provide real lessons for the investor because if I had followed my own rules, many losses could and should have been avoided.

These can be divided into four main categories:

1 Companies brought down by management/market failure where I had obviously over-rated the ability of individuals.

2 Companies where I failed to heed the warning signs.

3 Companies that were clearly drifting down and where I stayed aboard too long.

4 Companies where I just lost patience or tried to be too clever by buying as they were falling.

In the first category I put Leeds jewellery manufacturer Abbeycrest (see 'Jewellery shares acquire extra sparkle' below) and corporate clothing specialist Wensum (see the following article 'Tailored for both comfort and fit'), and also environmental services Fountains, and North West pigments etc. producer European Colour. In all cases the key individuals in whom I had faith sadly failed to deliver – they should have done much better, or probably reacted sooner to changes in their particular markets.

Jewellery shares acquire extra sparkle

John Lee discerns bright prospects for Abbeycrest behind the glitter of its product range

Leeds has been a happy hunting ground for me in recent years. Bray Technology was taken over for a good price and Town Centre Securities, a property developer based in the city, is showing a 40 per cent appreciation.

I was hoping for continued success as I prepared to attend the annual meeting of jewellery maker and distributor Abbeycrest.

I had already made a modest purchase of shares on the back of solid results, a good set of accounts, and favourable press comment. But I also wanted to check the company for myself.

The meeting was held at the city-centre office of Arthur Andersen, the company's auditors – not the most exciting venue. Even one of Abbeycrest's non-executive directors had wisely gone on holiday. But once the board had recovered from the shock of a shareholder actually turning up at the meeting, I was well received.

I was impressed to find that Michael Lever, chairman and chief executive, had himself started the business in 1979 – with a partner who has died. Twenty years later, a turnover of £70m, pre-tax profits of £5m and a personal shareholding worth £6m clearly point to a wise career move by Mr Lever, who was previously a dentist.

Lever and his team believe they have only just started the task of building Abbeycrest into a much larger international company. Although 85 per cent of its sales are in the UK through high street chains such as Signet, Goldsmiths, Debenhams and independent retailers, an increasing proportion is coming from the US and continental Europe. Wal-Mart, the giant US supermarket group, is now a customer.

The past year has seen a build-up of manufacturing capacity in Thailand and Hong Kong, and the purchase of a Teesside maker of bracelets and bangles.

An increase in production and assembly employees from 362 to 573 indicates the scale of change as Abbeycrest moves to owning more of its manufacturing capacity. Lever hopes this will bring greater management control, better customer service and higher margins.

The group is very focused on cash generation and bottom-line profitability. Even after the above expansion, gearing remains modest and the current 115p share price is fully backed by assets.

In spite of being in a rather bright and glitzy business, Lever is modest, conservative and cautious, albeit with ambition. This is an attitude which has clearly impressed institutional investors, which include Prudential, Legal & General, Hermes and Royal & SunAlliance. The institutions together own about half the equity of Abbeycrest.

There are just under 500 individual shareholders, among them Danny Fiszman, a big investor in Arsenal football club and a leading diamond trader. He has been steadily buying and is believed to own approaching 12 per cent. His intentions remain unclear.

All this makes Abbeycrest an intriguing and compelling proposition. In an age of increasing affluence and fashion consciousness, jewellery is clearly a growth sector. Abbeycrest is determined to be a force. Profits have increased steadily in recent years, even though they remain below the £6.8m peak achieved in the early 90s.

With the shares on a prospective p/e ratio of around seven, and with a three-times-covered dividend yield of just less than 5 per cent, I was confident enough on the return journey to phone my broker and add to my holding. Just my sort of share.

I hope that, following a little gentle chiding, next year's annual meeting will be brighter and better. I don't want to be the only shareholder there next time.

Source: Lee, J. (2000) Jewellery shares acquire extra sparkle, *Financial Times*, 5 August.

Tailored for both comfort and fit

John Lee finds that clothing company Wensum is an impressive corporate dresser

As an active investor for 40 years, and with an accountancy qualification, it usually takes me only a few minutes to form a view of a company as I work through its report and accounts.

The experienced eye knows what to look for, the statistics on which to focus, and which phrases convoy the key messages.

One does not always draw the right conclusions, of course – investment is not so easy – but going through a checklist should help to keep losses to a minimum.

Take the Norwich-based Wensum plc – one of my more recent purchases – and see why I formed a positive and favourable opinion.

I ask 10 questions, applying a score from one to 10 to each. The subject areas cover trade/activity, profits record, dividend yield and cover, asset backing, cash/borrowing, board shareholdings, institutional holdings, the price/earnings ratio, professional advisers/non-executive directors, and company optimism/brokers' forecasts.

In Wensum's case, and to assist clarity, I have blocked together the subject areas that I score the same. In three categories, I gave Wensum a score of seven. These are trade/activity, asset backing and cash/borrowing.

Although men's tailored clothing and corporate career wear (Wensum is No 1 in travel/leisure, supplying uniforms to groups such as Virgin) do not have the growth potential of internet stocks, the company's record and modest size points to further expansion.

On the issue of asset backing, shareholders' funds of £4.6m compare satisfactorily with the £6.8m market capitalisation. As for cash/

borrowing, Wensum is financed conservatively, being moderately cash-positive at the year-end.

Two categories achieved a score of eight: profits record and professional advisers/non-executives. Wensum has increased its earnings per share every year, from 9.14p in 1995 to 14.24p in 1999. And while it only has one non-executive director, comfort comes from the presence of auditor Ernst & Young, solicitor Eversheds and broker Williams de Broë.

In the higher-scoring areas, categories deserving a mark of nine were dividend yield and cover (a 6 per cent yield covered nearly three times is very acceptable), and institutional holdings (venture capitalist 3i Group has 15.9 per cent).

Wensum also scores a nine on company optimism/brokers' forecasts. According to the board: "Both divisions have excellent order books and have started the year well." Brokers are forecasting a rise in profits, from £1.54m to £1.73m, for the year to January 2000.

Finally, scores of 10 were achieved on two counts: board shareholdings and p/e ratio. Wensum's directors appear to own a constant 45 per cent of the equity, which demonstrates a deep, permanent commitment to the company.

The p/e of around six is exceptionally low for a solid and growing business.

When it comes to adding up the marks, my general conclusions are that any company achieving more than 90 out of 100 is an outstanding investment; 80-plus is very cheap – an excellent buying opportunity; 70-plus is good, but better value might be found elsewhere; and 60-plus is nothing special. Below 60? Forget it.

So, for Wensum, a total score of 84 (three sevens, two eights, three nines and a pair of 10s) out of a maximum of 100 says "buy".

Although it is a very small public limited company, with all the usual lack of liquidity in the shares, Wensum should provide substantial reward for the patient investor. Meanwhile, a rising 6 per cent dividend yield is worth having.

A final note. Wensum's board continues "to strongly believe that the company's share price does not reflect the underlying quality of, and prospects for, the business".

This is a view that I endorse happily. It has to be worth at least 50 per cent more.

Source: Lee, J. (1999) Tailored for both comfort and fit, *Financial Times*, 31 July.

Author note

Sadly, another management failure, with the company and my shareholding both going downhill. Embarrassingly, I paid up to 112p in 2006, finally selling out two years later for a measly 16p – frankly, a disaster. Here again a 20% stop-loss would have been damage limitation. In the article I quote the Wensum Board who continue 'to strongly believe that the company's share price does not reflect the underlying quality of, and prospects for, the business'.' Enough said. I am afraid they lost considerably more money than I did as they had substantial shareholdings themselves.

In the secondary category, where I failed to heed the warning signs, I have only myself to blame. Take software systems Jasmin (see 'On the scent of success at Jasmin' below). I wrote: 'Since 1998 the company has parted company with its nominated financial adviser, broker and auditor, not to mention an array of executive and non-executive directors. The group is on its fourth finance director since that date.' Even though I did say that Jasmin is 'definitely not a widows and orphans investment', warning lights were flashing – I really shouldn't have touched it with a barge pole. Hence now one of my guiding principles is 'stability of Board and advisers'.

On the scent of success at Jasmin

John Lee finds a software company making some shrewd moves amid top team changes

The Nottingham headquarters of software systems company Jasmin is protected by a heavy security gate. The gate has seen substantial activity in recent years. Since 1998 the company has parted company with its nominated financial adviser, broker and auditor, not to mention an array of executive and non-executive directors. The group is on its fourth finance director since that date.

It was these upheavals that concerned me when I first visited in 1999 after buying a modest holding. What would this year's annual meeting hold?

Jasmin is very much the creation of chairman and managing director Roger Plant, who founded it 30 years ago. He still owns about a third of the equity. Plant admits to being a hard taskmaster and setting high standards. He accepts that getting the right top team has not been easy.

What attracted me to Jasmin was a record of steady profits growth through the 1990s. What's more, the company had lived within its means, building conservatively. But fighting larger competitors eventually took its toll, as did heavy spending on R&D. Turnover dived to just over £4m for the year to March, producing a £1m loss. Gearing rose to 56 per cent.

Jasmin now accepts that, given its limited resources, it has to form strategic partnerships. Some of its likely partners remain commercially confidential. But relationships with WS Atkins (in traffic control systems) and Marconi Communications (a deal that involves developing readers for sophisticated new smartcards) say much for Jasmin's reputation.

Plant has shrewdly taken the company into a number of areas with potential. These include: passenger information displays for London Underground and Railtrack; airport ground lighting systems (with Jasmin now having preferred status with BAA for closed-circuit television); and city surveillance systems for local authorities. Each of these fields should see large increases in national spend, and many projects are being tendered for.

Jasmin has significant defence interests, working with the Ministry of Defence in simulation and biological and chemical detection systems.

I found a mood of optimism at the annual meeting, boosted by the company's new £10m contract with the National Highways Agency to upgrade all motorway emergency phones.

Jasmin is definitely not a "widows and orphans" investment, but my own portfolio is sufficiently solid to carry one or two "hope" stocks.

The current financial year will produce breakeven at best. But Jasmin could then begin to motor. Its broker, Old Mutual Securities, calculates that at the current price of 140p the shares are trading on a multiple of 6 times forecast earnings for 2002. This compares with a ratio of 50-plus on many software stocks.

With a current modest capitalisation of £7m, the brokers reckon that the potential for re-rating is "enormous". I am more cautious. There is a long way between a contract being won and its profitable and successful completion.

Jasmin must not over-stretch itself, and I would like to see a more settled board. Even so, I was sufficiently enthused by the annual meeting to add to my holding. My hunch is that Jasmin's time will come.

 Source: Lee, J. (2000) On the scent of success at Jasmin, *Financial Times*, 9 September.

Author note

While I did say that Jasmin was not a 'widows and orphans' investment, I still should have known better. Between 1998 and writing the article in 2000 they were on their fourth finance director. Even the dumbest of investors should have smelled a rat. Serves me right!

With both Aero Inventory and more recently HMV I was seduced by the double-figure yields on both, unfortunately ignoring the fundamentals. The former's business model appeared sound, holding a wide range of spare parts for airline operators, but it had a high level of debt – contrary to another of my guiding principles – and the investment community was clearly suspicious of it and gave it a very low market rating. Nevertheless, to this day its subsequent collapse remains something of a mystery.

With HMV it was rather different (see graph opposite), although here again there was a high level of debt. Of course, I was aware that more and more listeners were downloading their own music rather than buying CDs and also that internet purchasing was hitting HMV's sales, but I judged, rather naively, that some of the company's new technological products on which it was focusing would compensate. In addition, HMV owned what I thought was a valuable division, putting on live concerts. I also hoped that it would be able to negotiate lower shop rentals with landlords keen to retain the company as a tenant (something that the new owners of HMV are managing to do). I did visit two HMV stores. In truth, they should have been busier than they were and I should have known better. However, I ploughed on. I bought in July and August 2010 at just over 60p, finally facing up to my mistake in December of that year by selling at 35p. Painful, yes, but it would have been much, much worse if I had not cut my losses.

HMV

Offer for sale @ 160p 15/5/2002
Listing suspended 15/1/2013

— HMV HMV GRP ORD 1P

Source: Fidessa

This graph should have warned me off. I cut my losses, selling at 35p. Had I held on, my holding would have become virtually worthless

In the third category, staying on board for too long, as the companies got nowhere and went downhill, come printers Litho and window ventilation specialist Titon. In both cases my 20% stop-loss recommendation would have saved money had it been in operation. Both Litho and Titon had sizeable cash holdings, which did give me reassurance, but this did not prevent a steady drain.

The fourth category includes companies such as insurance industry investor/venture capitalist BP Marsh, which I just got tired with, waiting for 'value' to come through. I first invested in 2007 at just over 140p, departing at end-2009 at 75p. Only now, in 2013, is the value being recognised, with a share price north of 100p.

The subprime market crash of 2008 provided some splendid buying opportunities, but one was definitely not motor retailer Pendragon, which I bought after it had fallen heavily. Sadly, it fell further, leading to a painful disposal – bought at 19.5p, sold at 4.12p. Ouch!

I suppose that there is also a fifth category of loss: just plain bad luck. I had made a substantial profit on newspaper/periodicals distributor Dawson between 1993 and 1998 before starting to rebuild my holding in 2001, attracted by its 7–8% dividend yield, which appeared safe. The problem was that Dawson was the smallest of the three distributors in that industry, the other two being Smiths, now Smiths News, and John Menzies. They all competed for distribution contracts from the newspaper/periodical publishers. Unfortunately Dawson lost out when the contracts were put up for renegotiation and was virtually wiped out in a very short period. A considerable shock to myself and fellow investors. The company was left with just one or two small subsidiaries, including a library supplier.

> **❝ I suppose that there is also a fifth category of loss: just plain bad luck ❞**

In retrospect, Dawson should probably have merged with Menzies, thus competing jointly against Smiths, but this is of course with the benefit of hindsight. I lost substantially, more than wiping out earlier profits. Finally, the rump of Dawson was bought by Smiths. My only consolation was that subsequently, in 2011, I bought into Smiths News – itself on a near double-figure yield – and have virtually doubled my money, tax free within my ISA.

My successes

PEPs/ISAs

I have included in this chapter PEPs/ISAs and takeovers because many of my successes have been by way of takeovers and many of these have also been 'sheltered' – free of capital gains tax – within my PEPs/ISAs, thus there is an obvious inter-relationship. The *FT* article in December 2003 on me becoming a PEP/ISA millionaire, 'How I made £1m from £126,200', is fully reproduced at the end of this chapter, together with the linked Q&A, 'How can I do what he's done?'. The chapter works through my major successes on a chronological basis, culminating with a number of shares I currently own where I sit on large profits.

Chapter 3 details some of my initial activities when I was operating with very little capital. In the latter 1960s, as my resources grew slightly larger, I doubled my money on Brock Alarms, a 'long-term' profit of £217. (In those days capital gains tax differentiated between 'long-term' and 'short-term' gains, something I would like to see today.) Similarly, £177 on Slater Walker and a 'short-term' profit of £58 on supermarket new issue Amos Hinton.

By the 1970s I was investing larger sums: a profit of £400 on a £7,000 stake in holiday camp Pontins; £1,230 on a £4,400 holding in British Vita; and more than doubling my money on a £6,300 holding in car care products Holt Lloyd. It was in 1976 and 1977 that I made my first ever investments in overseas trader Paterson Zochonis, now PZ Cussons, and North West contractor/

developer Pochin's respectively – I refer to both in Chapter 4 covering family PLCs. More later on as I still hold both.

Takeover successes

This era also saw two takeover successes: a 25% profit on a £10,000 holding in Madame Tussauds in 1978, after a hard-fought battle between Pearson and ATV, and in the same year more than a 100% profit on bakery powders/specialist foodstuffs Goldrei Foucard. I was very fortunate here: I bought in June 1978, then went to the AGM of this family-controlled PLC in a London suburb, discovering that there was no apparent family succession. Lo and behold, by October an agreed takeover was announced.

This was an early example of a proprietorial or family PLC sell-ing out. Over the years many other similar companies have succumbed to bids where for a mix of reasons the controlling family decided to sell and realise the worth of their holdings. Often family shareholders not connected with the company in an executive capacity would rather realise a slug of capital to do their own thing – buy a better house, a farm, a yacht – than receive per-haps an annual dividend. And who can necessarily blame them – we only have one life.

I made fairly substantial profits on three larger family PLCs on holdings that I had patiently built up – Stockport bell chimes manufacturer Friedland Doggart, bought by MK Electric in 1985, small electrical appliances Pifco, taken over by Salton of the USA in 2001, and lights/switches/cable manufacturer GET by the French electrical group Schneider in 2006. The following two arti-cles tell the stories of Pifco and GET in more detail.

Years of patience pay off with Pifco

The £50m takeover by Salton Group is good news for long-term investor John Lee

Although the £50m takeover of electrical appliances manufacturer Pifco by Salton Group of the US is very pleasing to me financially, its demise is tinged with regret as it marks the end of a long-term investment relationship.

Pifco is one of those companies that can be described as a safe haven for my savings; it is a "proprietorial" plc, where a family effectively has managerial and equity control, usually stewarding conservatively.

Many of these companies are characterised as being cash-rich. Over the years dividends are steadily increased and the value of the business grows. But the stock market capitalisation lags well behind – through a combination of its low profile and limited marketability – often perceived to be boring by whizkid fund managers.

I first bought Pifco in 1976, subsequently taking useful profits on four occasions. They were also my first Pep investment in October 1987 when, after a long search, I finally discovered Midland Bank Trust Co, which allowed me to "self select".

Around half my current holding is historic, the balance being acquired in the latter 1990s.

I kept closely in touch with my investment through post-results announcements, phone discussions and AGM attendance – usually being the only attendee.

Pifco's big coup was the acquisition of loss-making Russell Hobbs, turning it round in double-quick time. However, it was in the classic small company dilemma. It either had to acquire or ultimately would be acquired, particularly as there was no family succession.

Kenwood was in its sights for a long time, but in the end wisely decided not to overstretch itself and enter an auction following an Italian bid.

I visited early last year before an article of mine appeared in the FT headed "Unloved, unwanted, undervalued" and written with Pifco shares at 135p. I wrote: "Pifco is clearly worth much more than its £24m capitalisation. I would be fascinated to hear just what valuation a brand consultant would place on it – there is also a large cash pile likely to be around £12m by year end."

During the early months of this year, the shares rose with "value" investor Fortress Finance steadily upping its stake to 7 per cent; then in April it was announced that it was in talks that could lead to an offer – a further bounce to £2.

I always believed that Pifco was worth nearer £3 than £2, and thus was happy with an agreed 276p. But even that was not a knockout price – a third party could enter the fray – so I bought a few more at 270p, there was no downside even with dealing costs.

While press comments referred to it as a "done deal" with 54 per cent "irrevocably accepted", in reality, from examination of the offer document, only the directors' 20 per cent was irrevocable. The balance had a "get out" in the event of another bidder offering 10 per cent more.

However, nobody else has appeared, so it is farewell my old friend at 276p. This represents a 150 per cent profit on cost for me, and as it was a significant holding, it's an excellent start to the new tax year for both myself and my partner the Inland Revenue.

There is a loan note alternative, but I prefer to take the cash, pay the tax – a third of my holding is held within Peps and is therefore free of CGT – and move on. There are other Pifcos out there, so happy hunting. Stock market value always comes through in the end.

 Source: Lee, J. (2001) Years of patience pay off with Pifco, *Financial Times*, 26 May.
© The Financial Times Limited 2001. All Rights Reserved.

Author note

My earlier article on Pifco ('Unloved, unwanted and undervalued') focused on its undervaluation and potential. Here I record its takeover by Salton of the USA, delivering me a handsome profit in 2001. However, I had held the shares since the mid-1980s – again patience paid off.

Patiently waiting for the end-game

John Lee

Over the years I have been on the receiving end of many profitable takeovers – indeed they, and the occasional management buyout, are invariably the end-game of my relationship with so many of my investments – rather akin to the passing of an old friend.

Of perhaps 40-plus existing small-cap holdings I would anticipate that broadly 80 per cent will have succumbed 10 years hence – probably 50 per cent within five years. In many ways one would prefer them to grow independently to become the mid-caps of the future. But the trend towards larger corporations in an era of increasing globalisation, the desire of family-controlled businesses to capitalise on personal wealth, perhaps because of the lack of family succession, and the frustrations with managing an unloved and undervalued plc, encourage takeover activity.

From personal experience the most profitable bids (in other words the biggest premiums on prevailing market prices) arise when a family controlled company is sold. Then comes the contested takeover with the management buyout a poor third, usually the lowest price that shareholders can be decently offered, leaving plenty in it for the buyout team and its backers!

For me the week of September 11 had it all; on Monday it was announced that family-controlled electrical products manufacturer/distributor Get had agreed a 260p cash offer from the giant French electrical group Schneider – a 73 per cent premium to the share price prior to bid talks being announced. Midweek came the news that the management of niche insurance broker Windsor was considering making a 52.5p offer – an 18 per cent premium to the prevailing price. And finally on Friday Biotrace, which makes contamination detection equipment for the food, beverage

Get
Share price (pence)

Source: Thomson Datastream

and defence sectors, rose 20 per cent on announcing that it had received a number of preliminary approaches.

My association with Get goes back to May 2001 when I made my first purchase at 157p following a visit to its large Midlands distribution depot where I met chairman John Joseph and financial director Michael Cohen. I bought more shares at between 117p and 203p over the next two years, mostly within my Pep, feeling that it was my type of solid well-stewarded business with every prospect of rising profits and dividends. All went well until 2005 when poor trading within their DIY sector and consequent high stock levels saw profits fall and a slashing of the dividend by over 50 per cent. I angrily clashed with them over this latter decision, believing it to be unnecessarily draconian, seriously damaging their credibility with investors. Sure enough the shares slumped to under 100p but I still had faith, buying more at 115p.

Unfortunately in March 2006 the company moved to Aim, the junior stock exchange, a very expensive decision for me as it transpired. I had to "buy out" the shares from my Peps at 103p (most Aim shares cannot be held in Peps or Isas) and thus I now face a thumping CGT liability on the 260p bid!

I started to buy Windsor in February 2002 at 22p after meeting chairman David Low at the company's AGM, steadily increasing my holding with 15 further purchases up to 43p – again predominantly sheltered in my Peps and Isas. Two sales were made at 39p in 2003 and 56p in May 2005. Profits, dividends and the share price rose steadily in the early years of ownership but recently overall performance has been more pedestrian, leaving the price somewhat becalmed on a single figure price/earnings ratio.

I cannot believe that Low and his buyout team, who after all give professional advice to others, would announce a likely precise price of 52.5p if they had not already lined up their financial backing. This modest price could well be topped by a trade buyer.

Biotrace, my only Welsh holding, has been this year's "find" and I have bought 13 lots at between 87p and 97.5p, all sheltered in Peps and Isas. I have written of the company as being significantly undervalued. 3M clearly agreed. This week the diversified technology company announced a recommended 130p per share cash bid for Biotrace – all very pleasing but – who knows? – other bidders may yet appear.

So all in all a very exciting week but the moral is clear: buy sound established profitable companies at the right price, put time into the equation and be patient. Value will always come through in the end.

Source: Lee, J. (2006) Patiently waiting for the end-game, *Financial Times*, 7 October.

Author note

Here we record the takeovers of GET and Biotrace, and the management buyout of Windsor. I would just like to emphasise and repeat the concluding sentences: '... but the moral is clear: buy sound established profitable companies at the right price, put time into the equation and be patient. Value will always come through in the end.'

Later on in this chapter I talk more about takeovers, how they arise, and the pros and cons from an investment standpoint.

In the 1980s I had many more successes than failures: textile group Coats Patons and cigarette manufacturer Rothmans (I would not buy a tobacco share today as a matter of principle), bought on very low single-figure price earnings ratios and good yields, both delivered £10,000+ profits; hostels/hotels Rowton nearly double that, and two early sales of PZ Cussons in 1981 and 1987 made profits totalling £25,000.

It was from gains like these that I was able to start building up some larger holdings. Local property company Trafford Park Estates (TPE) was a situation which caught my eye. As its name implies, it owned a substantial acreage of buildings, land, railway track, etc. in Manchester's Trafford Park industrial area, very close to the Manchester Ship Canal and adjacent to Manchester United's Old Trafford (TPE sold some land to the football club to facilitate ground expansion). The company was very conservatively run, the shares stood at a significant discount to assets, there were no controlling shareholders, and I was convinced that one day TPE would be taken over at a good price.

I first bought in 1990 at 62p, making 11 more purchases between then and 1996 at between 41p and 116p; some were made in my PEP. I used to follow TPE closely, reading all available comment and attending its AGMs. For some reason I sold a portion in 1997 at 140p and 168p. The takeover bid finally arrived one year later in 1998 at 190p from Irish property company Green. Unfortunately no other bidder appeared – a battle is ideally what you hope for at ever escalating prices – but here the first bid won the day. I had made my largest ever profit – a six-figure sum – of which two-thirds was taxable, one-third tax sheltered. The message is: 'Stick to your convictions' – don't be tempted to get out early from a good value holding.

> **" stick to your convictions – don't be tempted to get out early from a good value holding "**

Over the years property shares have served me well. 'Property has provided me with firm foundations' below talks of the successes I have had with several property companies over the years, including TPE and the Leeds-based Ziff family's property company, Town Centre Securities, owner of the Merrion Centre in that city. However, two rules: first, always buy property shares at a discount to net assets, and second, once again put time into the equation – be patient, your ship will eventually come home.

Property has provided me with firm foundations

John Lee

I first became aware of property shares 50 years ago, on reading an investment newsletter – I think it was written by a man called Beveridge – which my father used to receive. Beveridge extolled the virtues of Harold Samuel's Land Securities – and I much regret never having tucked some away.

My first property holding was developer Edger Investments – named from the ED of Edwin McAlpine and GER of City solicitor Gerald Glover. My records don't go back that far but I suspect my holding cost all of £100 – I cannot remember the outcome!

Over the years, I have bought and sold many property shares and been through several property peaks and troughs. Usually, I focused on lowly-geared plcs at a significant discount to assets – often finding this combination in family-dominated businesses.

While I have incurred one or two small losses – Warnford Estates in 1973–74 and Barlows in 1991-94 – property shares have served me well, which is not surprising given inflation and the general appreciation in property values.

This year marks the 50th anniversary of the Freshwater family's Daejan Holdings going public. The annual report tells us that, in 1959, net assets equated to 29p per share. Today, that figure is £46.60, a 160-fold increase! Sadly, I didn't buy until 2007, paying £41 per share, then £29 later that year and £27.50 in 2008.

The nearest I have come to a Daejan-like performance was with north-west building services company Pochins which, in recent years, was powered along by its property developments. I first invested in 1977 and then finally in 1984, with my average buying price being (an adjusted) 5p. The shares peaked at just over £4 in 2007 – I felt they were "toppy" and realised some at just under that figure. However, in the recent maelstrom, they have plunged to a current 85p – but still show me a 17-fold appreciation.

Another significant success was with industrial property owner Trafford Park Estates, which I bought on 12 separate occasions between 1990 and 1996 at 41p-116p. It was subsequently taken over by Green Properties of Ireland for 190p in 1998.

Other more modest successes included a 1996 purchase of London Industrial Group (later renamed Workspace), Peel Holdings – developer of The Trafford Centre – in 2000, Yorkshire small industrial estates owner Headway in 2001 (I remember getting lost in Halifax's one-way system searching for one of its sites!) and London landlord Estates and Agency Holdings in 2004.

However, the Ziff family's Leeds-based Town Centre Securities must be my all time yo-yo. I paid 64p in 1999 for a good yield and assets discount. By skilful management – including buying back half its equity – the NAV rose steadily, with the shares peaking at 653p in 2007. I sold some at 595p. The banking/property crisis then sent the shares crashing – I bought again at 60p in February 2009, selling three-quarters of this purchase at 182p in September – a trebling in seven months.

Today, I hold seven property stocks: Daejan, McKay, Pochins, Primary Health, Sovereign Reversions, Stewart & Wight and Town Centre. I regard them all as long-term "holds".

 Source: Lee, J. (2009) Property has provided me with firm foundations, *Financial Times*, 7 November.

Author note

Over the years I have done very well by investing in property shares, achieving some spectacular profits, but I always buy at a discount to net asset value. The rise and fall of Pochin's is chronicled in Chapter 4.

More on takeovers

In family PLCs, takeovers tend to happen when there is a lack of family succession or there is a desire to realise wealth. In non-controlled PLCs, i.e. where there are no controlling or dominant shareholders who could dismiss a takeover approach out of hand, takeovers usually involve a larger company taking over a smaller one. These latter takeovers are usually driven by the pressures of globalisation, a larger PLC seeking to 'take out' a troublesome competitor or to acquire a new revenue stream through diversification, perhaps a shortcut rather than developing itself through organic growth.

Sometimes directors of companies seek a takeover as a means of delivering value to shareholders or sometimes they wish to cash in their shareholdings/share options. Many commentators see takeovers as frequently destroying value in the acquiring company – a tendency to over-pay, perhaps resulting in the buyer taking on too much debt. What can be certain, however, is that in a free capitalist society takeovers will continue, they are a fact of commercial life. Personally, I would prefer a company to remain independent, ideally increasing its profits and dividends year on year, and this is arguably in the national interest as well. A takeover usually coming in at a premium on a prevailing market price delivers a certain profit to shareholders in the short term, but maybe at the expense of larger longer-term gain. Many criticise the short termism of the City, but in my experience most major UK financial institutions do take a longer view, although hedge funds and similar are usually more focused on the short term.

> ❝ in a free capitalist society takeovers will continue, they are a fact of commercial life ❞

There is a saying that a small cap stock is priced correctly only twice – on original flotation and on ultimate takeover; for the rest of its life it remains undervalued, thus offering the alert investor attractive buying opportunities. Over the years I have been on the receiving end of more than 40 bids, and only a handful have resulted in losses. Two I recall were large cap Cable & Wireless Worldwide – one of the Cable & Wireless twins – finally being put out of its shareholders' misery by Vodafone, and AIM-quoted tiddler James R. Knowles, in specialist arbitration/claims services to the international construction sector, bailed out by a US competitor. Unfortunately I was a non-executive director.

It is impossible to be absolutely certain that any particular company will be ultimately taken over, but as a generalisation, a small profitable PLC providing specialist services or products, particularly with a recognised brand name, is almost always going to attract predatory eyes at some stage. Another reason for preferring small caps.

Profitable takeovers for me included Jarvis Hotels, Norscot Hotels and Trust House Forte in the hospitality sector, Cheshire Whole Foods and Joseph Stocks in foods, THB and Windsor in insurance broking.

Windsor brings a touch of class

John Lee explains how he discovered a nugget in the smaller companies annual reports

Casting my eye over the smaller company annual reports in the Investors Chronicle – as always I was looking for new opportunities. I didn't spend too long on 7 Group – a "cash shell", Ninth Floor – "security technology and football club owner" or TZI "African producer of paper, batteries and roses". But what did catch my eye was insurance broker Windsor.

I looked more closely – steadily rising profits since a loss in 1997, a twice covered 5.5 per cent dividend yield, a price/earnings ratio of eight and the outlook described as "positive".

➡

Aware that insurance premiums had risen following September 11 with a consequent rise in brokers' shares, Windsor looked interesting and somewhat undervalued.

Over the weekend I searched the internet for any recent announcements, directors' share purchases and so on and carefully study my "bible" Company Refs. I found nothing negative – chairman and chief executive David Low's shareholding is a substantial and constant 12 per cent, almost equalled by Abtrust with Jupiter having nearly 6 per cent.

By a fortunate coincidence the annual meeting was in London the following Wednesday – I had a luncheon engagement in the West End that day – but I might just be able to look in as there was a noon start.

By Monday morning I had decided to "buy" and put a toe in the water – a call first thing to my broker and then one to Windsor's company secretary.

"Could I please have a copy of the annual report as soon as possible and what time does the agm start?" The answer to the latter was 10am. Although not usually a convenient time for me on this occasion it was perfect – I would definitely be there.

I decided to do more checking – and sought out anyone who knew anything about Windsor.

The company operates niche areas including sport and leisure, and professional indemnity. I found that friends running a large-scale visitor attraction used them and found them first class. But a fund manager I knew was aware that the executive team running the very successful professional indemnity business had an option to compel Windsor to "buy out" their substantial interest at any time – thus creating a degree of uncertainty in the minds of the investing community.

My annual report duly arrived in Tuesday's post – I studied it carefully as I travelled by train to London that afternoon. Wednesday found me at the company's Great Tower Street headquarters for the annual meeting.

I asked two questions during the formal meeting: on the re-appointment of the financial director – although he holds options does he plan to buy any shares as currently he owns none? Answer: No.

The chairman adds that the financial director is currently buying a house. Later – were the professional indemnity team "tied in" to continuing to work for Windsor in the event of them exercising their "put" option? Answer: a complicated issue but in all probability "Yes".

I lingered afterwards over coffee talking to David Low and his team and I got the feeling of a tightly run ship with further growth and expansion ahead – not fully recognised in the then £12m capitalisation at 22p.

I didn't depart until noon – only just making my luncheon engagement! It had been a whirlwind romance – I have subsequently added to my holding at a slightly higher price – the market is tight. Windsor now sit snugly in my portfolio – another stock "put down" for the future.

 Source: Lee, J. (2002) Windsor brings a touch of class, *Financial Times*, 2 March.
© The Financial Times Limited 2002. All Rights Reserved.

Author note

Here I tell the story of how I first alighted on insurance broker Windsor through reading an article in Investors Chronicle and how I then checked it out. AGM attendance provided useful confirmation. While the ultimate buyout was profitable, it was not a bonanza – buyouts rarely are as Boards/management obviously pay the minimum price they can get away with.

Other takeover successes included Parkdean in caravan parks, Gibbs and Dandy in builders' merchants, Broadcastle, Hitachi and Wintrust in specialist finance, Breedon in quarrying, Ben Bailey in housebuilding; thankfully just before the 2008 subprime crash, Sovereign Reversions and Peel Holdings in property, Refuge in insurance, and Wyevale in garden centres.

Exchange of ideas

Capital Pub is a more recent success story and an exceptionally profitable one. I first heard of it at an investment dining club of which I am a member. We operate a small, somewhat speculative portfolio, discuss investment ideas, and dine very well and convivially, usually at the Turf Club in London. Being a member of an investment club or similar is to be encouraged. Here we have a dialogue for mutual benefit where investment suggestions are

> **we have a dialogue for mutual benefit where investment suggestions are made**

made and a private investor finds thoughts and ideas considered and tested by their peers.

While many investors operate on their own – certainly in the ultimate making of decisions – most have a number of investing friends, as I have, among whom ideas and thoughts are exchanged, preferably over a good meal. A number of groupings of private investors have been formed in recent years. For example, www.sharesoc.org, with 3,000 members, takes up investors' grievances, and www.mellomeeting.co.uk, with over 800 members, arranges regular company presentations.

Capital, I learned, was building up a chain of quality freehold London pubs, significantly upgrading the food offering, and clearly benefiting from London's buoyant visitor economy. It sounded like my type of investment – worth investigating further. I lunched with Board members at their valuable Ladbroke Arms Hostelry and they impressed me as a focused and experienced management team.

I first bought in December 2009 at 70p, adding more the following year at 76p. I followed their progress with keen interest. It seemed obvious to me that at some stage Capital would be a very attractive add-on for a larger pub chain. Midway through 2011 it happened. Press reports indicated predatory interest. Finally a recommended bid came in from brewers Greene King. I sold my holding at just over 230p for a near six-figure profit. As Capital was an AIM stock (quoted on the Alternative Investment Market) it had been regrettably ineligible for my ISA. Thus a 28% share of my profit went to HM Revenue & Customs, but I must not be ungrateful – Capital had delivered an excellent profit in a far shorter period than usual.

Taxing issues

I now turn to the importance to me of my PEPs/ISA opportunities and how I have used the exemption from income tax and capital gains tax to advantage. The Thatcher government, of which I was a member, introduced personal equity plans in 1987. Individuals were allowed to invest an amount of money each year in shares (the limit changed on a number of occasions). You could either choose personally which holdings to invest in – I always did – or have your shares selected/managed by a PEPs manager. I viewed all this as an outstanding investment/savings opportunity.

> **❝ I viewed all this as an outstanding investment/savings opportunity ❞**

For the next 17 years I invested the maximum allowance every year, re-investing all dividends and tax credits received. The shares I bought had to satisfy all my normal criteria, but given the dividends' tax-free status, they assumed even greater importance. By December 2003 I had invested a grand total of £126,200, plus dividends re-invested, and at that time I wrote an article in the weekend *Financial Times* disclosing that the value of my PEPs/ISA portfolio had reached the magic £1 million. (The Labour government introduced ISAs to replace PEPs, but for all practical purposes they are essentially the same.) My full PEPs/ISA portfolio – reprinted in this article – was published, disclosing a value of £1,015,843.65. It included PZ Cussons, S&U, Nichols, Treatt, Christie Group, Air Partner and Primary Health Properties, most of which I still hold. However, Nichols and Christie moved from the main market to AIM, thus becoming ineligible for ISAs, so I had to 'buy out' these holdings; however, now that AIM stocks are eligible for ISAs, Christie have gone back in!

I continued to invest annually in my ISA for a number of years post-2003, but more recently with the overall value of my ISA thankfully moving further ahead I have stopped topping it up; clearly, as the ISA rose, a limited annual allowance became less relevant. My ISA is administered by the well-regarded firm of James Sharp in Bury, Greater Manchester, very much an old-style, traditional broker.

My basic principles

I now come to what in many ways is the raison d'être for this personal story and the main message that I wish to convey: that a substantial portfolio can be built, brick by brick, by applying common sense and basic investment principles. But it does take time! Hence 'how to make a million – slowly'.

I think the best way to demonstrate all this is to look at my holdings in May 2013 and see when I first bought into them. The article 'Proof I'm in it for the long haul' clearly emphasises in the summary, 'Through the years', why I regard myself as a serious long-term investor.

Proof I'm in it for the long haul

John Lee

For me, a private investor is someone who buys into a company, stays with it, and hopefully sees it prosper. A trader who regards the stock market as the equivalent of a short-stay car park – in and out as quickly as possible – is certainly not an "investor".

As someone in the former category, I thought it would be interesting to look into the duration of my shareholdings.

As a starting point, I took my first purchase of a serious current holding: toiletries group PZ Cussons, which I bought in 1976.

In 1977 came North West building services/property developer Pochin's; in 1994 I bought into both short-term lender S&U and pharmaceuticals distributor United Drug. The table shows my portfolio by year of purchase.

Many positions have been added to over the years, always with a view to the long term. Pleasingly, the majority are in positive territory – some spectacularly so – eg. PZ Cussons, with James Fisher, Nichols and Fenner appreciating substantially.

Pochin's has been a real roller coaster – rising to nearly £4 in 2007 – thankfully I sold some then – before sinking to a current 23p on joint venture property development horrors and concrete pumping losses.

Thankfully, my only real dog, Cable & Wireless Communications, is off the bottom.

These days I rarely make big changes, occasionally initiating a new position while benefiting from the healthy dividend flow. I tend to reinvest dividends; in my Isa, which houses 14 of the 30 holdings. All dividends are used to buy more shares.

I rarely sell out of shares completely, partly because many of my holdings aren't very liquid, and partly because I don't want to pay capital gains tax (shorn of indexation relief) at 28 per cent. But I often add to them; last month I added more Air Partner, which has loads of cash and offers a 6.5 per cent yield.

Through the years

1976: PZ Cussons (PZC)

1977: Pochin's (PCH)

1994: S&U (SUS); United Drug (UDG)

1999: Air Partner (AIP); Ensor (ESR); Treatt (TET)

2000: James Fisher (FSJ)

2002: Christie (CTG); Nichols (NICL)

2003: Wynnstay (WYN); Primary Health Properties (PHP)

2004: Gooch & Housego (GHH)

2005: Quarto (QRT)

2006: FW Thorpe (TFW); Delcam (DLC)

2007: Northbridge (NBI); Park Group (PKG); Daejan (DJAN)

2008: BBA (BBA); Fenner (FENR)

2009: Concurrent Technologies (CNC); Dairy Crest (DCG)

2010: VP (VP); Cable & Wireless Comms (CWC)

2011: Smiths News (NWS); Vianet (VNET); Balfour Beatty (BBY)

2012: Charles Taylor (CTR); Anpario (ANP)

Author note

Here is further evidence of my long-term investing and the exercise of patience. Most of my holdings tend to be long fused, i.e. usually I hold them for a number of years before they hopefully 'explode' into profit. Some have already delivered sizeable gains, like PZ Cussons, James Fisher, Delcam and Fenner. However, for Charles Taylor, Christie, Concurrent Technologies, Quarto and Vianet, hopefully their best is yet to come.

I have referred to my two long-held holdings PZC and Pochin's earlier in Chapter 4. PZC is a 'core' holding, an outstanding success story which has done me proud. Today it is one of my most valuable holdings, having delivered substantial capital and income growth.

One thing that all analysts and commentators accept is the importance of dividends and dividend growth and where possible, as in an ISA, the tax-free reinvestment of dividend income. Unfortunately, PZC is not in my ISA, therefore I receive and pay tax on its dividends. However, I am currently receiving a near-annual rising dividend yield of approximately 38% on my original cost price.

My other current 1970s' purchase, Pochin's, has sadly become a problem child in recent years and there is a question mark over its future. Currently it pays no dividend and has fallen dramatically from its peak. Even now though, the 'rump' is five times my original cost price and earlier sales have recouped more than the amount I invested. Nevertheless, at peak, in the boom times, my Pochin's holding alone was worth north of £1 million, but sadly that is history.

I held both short-term lender S&U and Irish/UK pharmaceutical distributor and packager United Drug for nearly 20 years. I have taken profits on the former family PLC over the years. My cheapest purchase was 290p in 1995, today they are around £13; the latter have appreciated six-fold.

Treatt, in flavours and fragrances, has been with me for 14 years. I have bought into it no less than 25 times, mainly in my PEPs/ISA, having paid between 153p in 1999 and 280p for my last purchase in 2006. Today – August 2013 – it is 630p, so a very nice gain. I have visited its Bury St Edmunds' base on two or three occasions and I have had numerous conversations with former chairman Hugo Bovill, and other executives. Its US division, started from scratch, is now probably more important than its UK base. It has also paid a steadily rising dividend over time. I always believed that Treatt was a very valuable business, unique to the stock market.

I briefly touched on marine services James Fisher in Chapter 7 because I wish that I had retained all my Fisher shares and had stayed aboard for the whole voyage rather than shedding shares at different ports, because Fisher has been a great success story (see 'All aboard for growth at the new Fisher' opposite).

All aboard for growth at the new Fisher

John Lee describes the attractions of investing in a traditional shipowner which is evolving its fleet into niche activities

My holiday reading this year included *Around the Coast and Across the Seas* by Nigel Watson. a fascinating history of shipowner James Fisher.

The company was founded in 1847, its growth built on the export of iron ore from Barrow-in-Furness, Cumbria. A stock exchange flotation came in 1881.

The circular enticing potential investors with news of a new ship costing £1,800 boasted: "We have had two of this class of vessel built lately and both have done and are doing well. We shall be glad to put your name down as a shareholder".

I wonder what today's regulatory authorities would make of the rather thin prospectus.

My first encounter with the company was in the early 1970s when the Manchester Dry Docks Company, where I was a director, repaired a number of James Fisher vessels. It was not until this year, however, that I became a Fisher shareholder.

James Fisher
Share price (pence)

Source: Thomson Financial Datastream

The company is unique in a number of ways. It is the UK's last quoted true shipowner. It expects to pay a tax rate of only 5 per cent for the foreseeable future as a result of the new tonnage tax regulations. It donates money to both the Conservative and Labour parties.

The Fisher family still retains an interest of about 25 per cent, owned through a charitable foundation, but the management is in the hands of David Cobb, a canny Scot with long experience in shipping. He has been at the helm since 1994 and is moving the fleet away from its traditional small tanker and dry cargo operations into rather more profitable niche activities.

For example, following excellent results from its cable layer Nexus, two more vessels have been purchased and are being converted in Croatia for delivery early next year.

They have been chartered for a minimum of five years by International Telecom USA, guaranteed by its parent General Dynamics, the US industrial group.

This represents a serious investment for James Fisher. The £40m cost is almost equal to the group's stock market value and compares with a net asset value of £70m. Fisher could be a surprising beneficiary of the global telecommunications boom.

Other specialist ships in the fleet include RFA Oakleaf, chartered to the Ministry of Defence, and New Generation, a roll-on-roll-off heavy lift vessel.

There is also a diving support ship, a joint venture with Cammell Laird. Two other James Fisher vessels carry irradiated fuel rods between British Nuclear Fuels and Japan.

The group has a business based in Aberdeen serving North Sea oil and gas production facilities. This is part of an Underwater Services division.

Fisher also manages an aircraft spares facility at RAF Sealand near Chester, and is the preferred bidder in a consortium with Bibby and Andrew Weir for a 20-year contract to operate six roll-on-roll-off ferries for the MoD.

The "new" James Fisher being shaped by David Cobb is therefore moving away from its roots as a traditional coastal shipper. That said, the transformation will take time. There is still a 30-strong James Fisher fleet of small tankers and dry cargo vessels. The latter are unprofitable.

Pre-tax profits sank from £8.7m to £3.8m in 1998, reflecting closure costs, but recovered to £6.2m last year. The performance of the shares has reflected these changing fortunes – hitting a peak of more than 150p in 1997 before falling back to a low this year of 63.5p.

Several factors persuaded me to invest. The minimal tax charge suggests scope for further dividend increases. The pay-out was increased by 16 per cent in 1999, and by a further 10 per cent at the interim stage in September.

The price-earnings ratio is very low at about five times this year's forecast earnings – despite the likely boost to profits from the two new cable layers over the next few years.

Even allowing for the fact that forecasts for this year have had to be trimmed – to take account of increased running costs arising from higher oil prices – the shares are hardly expensive. In the meantime, the yield is a comforting 5 per cent.

Sure enough, the shares have climbed towards 90p since the summer, helped by occasional bid speculation. It seems a good time for medium to long-term investors like me to come aboard what is a rather special company.

Source: Lee, J. (2000) All aboard for growth at the new Fisher, *Financial Times*, 28 October.
© The Financial Times Limited 2000. All Rights Reserved.

Author note

We end with me boarding marine services James Fisher in 2000 on a 'double five' – a yield of 5% and a price earnings ratio also of 5. Here again one can hardly go wrong at these levels, but a unique combination of organic growth coupled with shrewd niche acquisitions made Fisher an outstanding success – a 'ten bagger'+! I refer to Fisher in Chapter 7, 'My mistakes', because I took profits far too early. Easy to say this in retrospect – hindsight is a wonderful thing and never more so than in stock market investing.

I first bought in 2000, when the company primarily comprised a small fleet of coastal oil tankers, at 78p – more at 71p and 74p – but most acquired in 2000–3 at an average around 150p. I think people regard shipping as a rather staid sector, as I did initially. In fact, it has shown steady growth over the years, albeit with varying profitability through numerous shipping cycles. However, Fisher has steered clear of mainstream shipping, focusing on niche areas in marine services, such as sub-sea technology globally, and in the UK being involved in operating, at one time, our national submarine rescue service. It has grown organically and by numerous 'bolt-on' acquisitions, most of which have been successfully integrated.

Surprisingly, it would appear that no other PLC has copied Fisher's strategy in the marine sector. However, it has not all been plain sailing for the company – an early foray into cable-laying vessels was an expensive failure – but overall there have been far more correct calls. Today Fisher shares hover around £11. Thankfully I retain a significant minority of my original holding; I show 14-fold appreciation on my purchases, with a current 24% dividend return on cost.

The fourth of my major current holdings after Nichols, PZC and Treatt is software specialist Delcam. A former stockbroking colleague mentioned this company to me years ago at a Christmas party, observing that it was spending £9 million per annum on research and development but declaring a bottom line of profit of only approximately £1 million.

I decided to investigate further and visit its Birmingham base. There I discovered a superb, conservative business, quietly developing its specialist software for the manufacture globally of large shapes. Delcam had built up an international operation, with staff and agents throughout the world, and was clearly highly regarded. It is still the only business that I have come across which has built accommodation and a conference centre for its overseas employees and visitors on the small industrial estate where it is headquartered.

I first bought in 2006 at just over £3, in total making 16 purchases between 225p and 420p. Along the way rated PLC Renishaw encouragingly subscribed for 20% of Delcam's capital at £4 a share. In recent years the company has continued to invest substantially in R&D and developing overseas, but bottom-line profits have really started to come through and dividends have risen accordingly. The shares have recently touched £14.

Other noteworthy successes include Ilminster's electro-optical laser specialist Gooch & Housego, which have quadrupled, and Birkenhead voucher redemption group Park, which have trebled, as have Redditch lighting manufacturer F. W. Thorpe – all AIM quoted. In my ISA, conveyor-belting manufacturer Fenner holds top spot, having risen six-fold despite falling back to the 350p level from a peak of £5.

All these stocks are still very firmly held. In almost every case they have achieved the double whammy which I referred to earlier: real profits growth plus a re-rating.

So, the overall message is to take the long-term view – in the words of St Augustine, patience is the companion of wisdom.

How I made £1m from £126,200

John Lee believes many investors are missing out on the benefits offered by tax-free wrappers

I'm glad MPs aren't barred from benefitting from legislation they supported. If they were, I could be more than £1m poorer.

I have always been a devotee of the stock market and a disciple of long-term investment. So as Conservative MP for Pendle, and as a minister from 1983 to 1989, I firmly supported the creation of personal equity plans (Peps) by Margaret Thatcher's government in 1987.

For the first time, Peps gave everyone the opportunity to build a fund of equity investments free from income tax and capital gains tax. It was obvious that this was a great opportunity for serious savers, but I suspect that few recognised the golden potential.

For the next 17 years I invested the maximum allowance every year, reinvesting all dividends and tax credits received – less the Pep managers' charges, of course.

The ceiling on investment has changed several times. From 1987 to April 1991 I invested a total of £19,200, and from then to 1999 a further £72,000 – £6,000 a year in so-called general Peps and £3,000 a year in single company Peps. I kept investing the maximum allowed when

➡

Labour replaced Peps with individual saving accounts in 1999, and I have now invested £35,000 in Isas at £7,000 a year.

That makes a grand total of £126,200 invested since 1987, some of which I funded by selling shares in my main portfolio, which of course, is subject to both income tax and CGT.

Looking through my files, I find that I have generated no fewer than 463 contract notes, but the effort has been well worth it. When I had my Peps and Isas portfolio valued for this article earlier this month it was worth £1,015,843. In spite of the stock market crash in 2001, the average annual return is about 21 per cent.

My investing strategy has never varied. My first Pep investment, back in 1987, was in Pifco, the Manchester-based electrical appliance manufacturer. It was typical of the type of company to which my "DVY" approach – defensive value, plus yield – has always attracted me. It had valuable brands, a big proprietorial/family shareholding, and it was cash-positive with a history of profitability and rising dividends.

In addition, it was a small cap company and I judged it very likely to be on the receiving end of a takeover from a larger player one day. It was, very profitably for me, 14 years later.

As a small cap specialist I take a great deal of care over stock selection, researching the targets thoroughly, getting to know the managements wherever possible, and attending annual meetings whenever I can.

On many occasions I have been the only attending shareholder, which at least offers the chance of an uninterrupted dialogue with the board. On one occasion I was even offered a non-executive directorship, which I accepted.

Of course, not all my selections have been successful. I have had my misjudgements and disappointments. But where I have got it wrong I have usually acted speedily and decisively; the tax advantages of Peps and Isas are just too valuable to squander.

Thankfully, I have had many more successes than failures over the years, and I have benefited from a number of takeovers of companies in which I held a signature number of shares, including Bridport, Breedon and Trafford Park Estates as well as Pifco.

I have taken numerous tax-free profits by selling from my Peps and Isas shares that are performing well while retaining exposure to any further upside in my main portfolio. Most recently, I have done this with James Fisher and Lookers. Among my current favourites are Clarkson, Jarvis Hotels, P.Z. Cussons, Thorntons, Titon, Windsor and Wintrust.

I don't know whether I am the first private investor to build up a portfolio worth £1m in Peps and Isas. Perhaps I am only the first newspaper columnist to do so. But I do feel that most investors have not taken the taxation advantages of these vehicles on board.

The wealthy seem to regard them as a rather pointless chore, perhaps because they think that the investment ceilings are too low to justify the efforts involved. The less well-heeled tend towards a rather inconsistent approach, investing in some years but not in others, and often holding on to poorly performing shares long after they should have been dumped.

Both these approaches are wrong. If funds allow, the key is to invest the maximum amount every year, reinvest all dividends and keep a close eye on your holdings to make sure your average returns are not depressed by a few poor stocks.

Investors need to remember that, in the eyes of the Inland Revenue, Peps and Isas are divorced from any other holdings you may have. This means it is possible, for example, to create a loss in your main portfolio, off-setting it against other taxable profits, and then buy back the same stock in your Peps and Isas portfolio, ensuring that the profit from any future recovery is tax-free.

Those who think that investing in this way has its tedious side are not entirely wrong. One of the worst irritations is that companies quoted on the Alternative Investment Market (Aim) cannot be held in Peps and Isas.

This means that when a company leaves the main market for Aim – usually to save costs or to benefit from lighter regulation – the shares have to be sold. Obviously, they can be repurchased for the investor's main portfolio, but the tax advantages are lost. This is a manoeuvre I have carried out with several companies including Samuel Heath and Rowe Evans.

I have never worried too much about the costs of investing. In my view this pales into insignificance against the main issue, which is choosing the right stocks. I pay normal transaction costs plus a 0.5 per cent (plus value-added tax) manager's charge on the capital value of most of the Pepsas. This is more than covered by my current overall dividend yield of 4.5 per cent – leaving about 4 per cent for dividend reinvestment.

Gordon Brown, the chancellor, confirmed in his pre-Budget report last week that Isas are set to become rather less tax efficient. The 10 per cent tax credit on dividends is to be withdrawn in April, and the annual investment allowance is to fall from £7,000 to £5,000 in April 2006.

➡

I think this is a retrograde step. These measures will make only a small difference to Treasury revenue, and they are bound to discourage many people from using Isas, which seems illogical given that they are supposed to encourage saving.

But I think the benefits remain well worth having, particularly if you have already built up a sizeable nest egg. I intend to carry on very much as before, building my portfolios brick by brick, analysing, researching, visiting, always seeking to improve performance.

I'm currently interested in Jarvis Hotels and Thorntons, the chocolate maker, both of which are in play with management buy-outs mooted. I hope that both will generate profits and cash for reinvestment early next year.

Inevitably, the recovery in the market that lifted my Peps and Isas to the £1m level has brought yields down and made bargains much less easy to find. But 45 years of investing have taught me that there are always opportunities out there.

Not much changes, really. The two main ingredients of successful investing remain common sense and, above all, patience. My book about investing, if I ever get it finished, will be called *Making a Million – Slowly*.

Source: Lee, J. (2003) How I made £1m from £126,200, *Financial Times*, 20 December.

How can I do what he's done?

Lucy Warwick-Ching

Can't I just win £1m on the lottery and put it into an Isa?

Inland Revenue rules say you can put only £7,000 into a maxi stocks and shares Isa each year or £3,000 into a mini cash Isa. To become an Isa millionaire you would need to put the maximum amount in each year, play the markets and hope your shares perform well enough to give the value of your portfolio a strong and frequent boost.

If £7,000 a year is the top whack, how has John Lee managed it? He must have been investing for centuries.

He started investing in these tax-free products when they were launched in 1987 as personal equity plans (Peps). He invested the maximum all the way and carried on when Isas replaced Peps in 1999.

So he has paid in a total of £126,200 since Peps were launched.

Mine's a million
John Lee's portfoio

Company	No. of shares	Market Value (£)	Gain/loss (£)*
PZ Cussons	4,300	43,107.50	30,592.69
Clarkson	2,250	10,068.75	6,129.76
Windsor	54,500	23,026.25	8,302.08
S&U Ord	3,100	16,507.50	3,052.99
Titon Holdings	22,500	29,250.00	9,376.27
GET Group	21,500	43,215.00	15,919.19
Slingsby (HC)	4,250	25,925.00	4,633.27
Abbeycrest	40,775	28,746.38	−1,209.82
Nichols	15,450	21,089.25	4,459.22
Treatt	14,500	29,580.00	2,695.14
PZ Cussons	4,000	40,100.00	22,416.50
Jarvis Hotels	40,296	60,242.52	11,744.64
Christie Group	138,500	92,102.50	43,831.96
Air Partner	7,050	27,495.00	4,082.43
Clarkson	23,250	104,043.75	56,634.20
Thorntons	15,300	23,485.50	−1,880.24
Windsor	108,000	45,630.00	15,099.13
Wintrust	12,130	60,346.75	12,226.62
UCM	17,900	14,768.00	1,252.00
600 Group	22,500	13,669.00	1,268.00
Jarvis Hotels	42,450	63,463.00	2,380.00
Clarkson	25,000	106,000.00	3,996.00
Wintrust	2,700	13,433.00	661.00
Primary Health Properties	5,000	10,825.00	500.00
Others less than £10,000		69,724.00	756.00
Total		1,015,843.65	258,919.03

Source: John Lee

*Profit and loss figures do not reflect transactions on holdings no longer in the portfolio

So if I invest in Isas for the next 16 years, the same amount of time as he did, could I become an Isa millionaire?

Giles Pidcock, managing director of Baxter Fensham Financial Planning, says: "If you paid £7,000 every year into an equity Isa for the next 17 years, you would need a return of 21.09 per cent on your investments to make a million."

If this sounds like a tall order, Pidcock suggests clubbing together with your partner because you'll be able to double the amount you can invest to £14,000 a year. "If you do it together you would only need a return of 14.56 per cent to achieve the million," says Pidcock.

➡

That still seems an awful lot, especially in the present state of stock markets.

It's even harder than that I'm afraid. From 2007 the most that can be invested in an Isa will be cut from £7,000 a year to £5,000. The amount that can be put into a cash Isa will be cut from £3,000 to just £1,000.

My portfolio will have to work hard, then. Is there anything that's likely to outperform other stocks?

Meera Patel, senior analyst at Hargreaves Lansdown, says: "The biggest mistake people make is to buy high and sell low. Many people simply end up putting their money in the most fashionable funds promoted by investment firms. But as technology shareholders found out to their cost in the late 1990s, investing in funds that are the flavour of the month is a recipe for disaster. The way to make money is to be contrarian."

She says UK and other European stock markets are still much lower than they were in 1999. "Now is a good time to put your money in."

Pidcock says investors who want to become Isa millionaires will need to be aggressive. "You will need a lot of luck as well as taking on greater risk. Areas to invest in include smaller companies, sector-based and emerging markets funds."

Does it make much difference how I invest? Could I, for example, find my money being eaten up by charges?

Pidcock says one of the biggest drags on investment returns is the annual management charge, which can range from 1 per cent to 5 per cent.

The best way to invest in several funds is through fund supermarkets, which have greatly reduced charges. Even if you are investing in only one fund, the initial charge is usually cut by 2 or 3 per cent if you invest via a supermarket, and in some cases may be removed.

Some independent financial advisers also offer their own supermarkets where you can buy funds, without advice, at discounted prices. They include Chelsea Financial Services, Bates Investment, Hargreaves Lansdown, Chase de Vere and Charcol.

How can I make my money work harder to achieve high returns?

Advisers suggest spreading your money across a range of markets and investing in funds with different styles. But how you go about it depends largely on your attitude to risk. "If your sole aim is to try to become an Isa millionaire, you should be more adventurous because the risk of investing in volatile areas such as emerging markets and smaller companies may pay off over the longer term," says Patel.

It all sounds a bit more feasible, but are there any further problems.

There is an inheritance tax issue, I'm afraid. Pep and Isa money cannot be held within a trust. This means your £1m investment will be subject to IHT when you die. "Most assets can be placed in a trust, but not Isas or Tessas because they already attract tax relief," says Pidcock. "For example, if you did not own a house, the first £255,000 of your Isa and pep portfolio would be free from tax, but the rest would be subject to 40 per cent tax if you are a higher rate taxpayer."

Is there anything else?

Once the 10 per cent tax credit that equity Isas can currently claim on dividend income is abolished from April 2004, the case for saving within an equity Isa also becomes weaker.

Source: Warwick-Ching, L. (2003) How can I do what he's done?, *Financial Times*, 21 December.

Index

Get more for your money
with *Smarter Investing*